# Mind Twisters, Puzzles and Games

(Elementary – Intermediate)

Anna Southern and

Adrian Wallwork

# Contents

### ★ Students with 3 – 12 months of English

| Activity | Language point | Time (minutes) | Page |
|---|---|---|---|
| 1 Classroom | alphabet | 15 | 22 |
| 2 Countries | nouns, adjectives | 20 | 23 |
| 3 The time | *to be* | 20 | 24 |
| 4 Colours | ordinal numbers | 15 | 25 |
| 5 The calendar | dates | 10 | 26 |
| 6 Spot the difference | *there is, there are, how many?* | 15 | 27/28 |
| 7 Habits | present simple, *can* | 30 | 29 |
| 8 The human face | possessives | 15 | 30 |
| 9 Rooms | *there is, there are* | 30 | 31 |
| 10 Picture puzzles | following instructions | 15 | 32 |
| 11 Smileys | keyboard characters, *looks like* | 15 | 33 |
| 12 Quantities | *not…enough, too* | 15 | 34 |
| 13 Geography | comparisons | 15 | 35 |
| 14 Food and drink | *how much? how many?* | 15 | 36/37 |
| 15 Crazy conundrums | prepositions of place | 15 | 38 |

### ★★ Students with 1 – 2 years of English

| Activity | Language point | Time (minutes) | Page |
|---|---|---|---|
| 16 Family members | male *vs* female | 30 | 39 |
| 17 Jail break | *can, must* | 15 | 40 |
| 18 Coin game | *can, must* | 15 | 41 |
| 19 Work it out | opinions | 15 | 42 |
| 20 Numbers | *must* | 15 | 43 |
| 21 School bus | *some, any* | 15 | 44 |
| 22 Guess the object | *it vs one* | 15 | 45 |
| 23 Experiences | superlatives, present perfect | 30 | 46 |
| 24 High numbers | *will* | 30 | 47/48 |
| 25 Number games | imperative | 15 | 49/50 |
| 26 Farmer's dilemma | first conditional | 20 | 51 |
| 27 School jokes | *can, can't* | 20 | 52 |

| Activity | Language point | Time (minutes) | Page |
|---|---|---|---|
| 28 Teacher jokes | present simple, present continuous | 20 | 53 |
| 29 Lift mystery | present simple | 15 | 54 |
| 30 Chatline acronyms | present continuous | 15 | 55 |
| 31 Riddles | present simple | 15 | 56 |
| 32 Giving directions | imperative | 30 | 57 |
| 33 Ask the teacher | irregular verbs, past simple, present perfect | 20 | 58 |
| 34 Visual game | following instructions | 20 | 59 |
| 35 Horse race | irregular verbs | 15 | 60 |
| 36 Maths | first conditional and temporal clauses | 15 | 61 |
| 37 Silly maths | quantities | 15 | 62 |
| 38 Text messaging | present simple | 15 | 63 |

## ★★★ Students with 2 – 3 years of English

| Activity | Language point | Time (minutes) | Page |
|---|---|---|---|
| 39 Loch Ness Monster | active / passive | 15 | 64 |
| 40 Night watchman | past simple, past continuous | 15 | 65 |
| 41 Beastly brainteasers | following instructions | 20 | 66 |
| 42 Detectives | past simple, past perfect | 15 | 67 |
| 43 Hotel mystery | past simple, past continuous | 20 | 68 |
| 44 Doctor jokes | imperative | 20 | 69 |
| 45 Crack the code | present simple, present perfect | 30 | 70 |
| 46 English humour | past simple, present perfect | 10 | 71 |
| 47 Shoe mystery | present continuous, past simple | 20 | 72 |
| 48 School facilities | *should*, *need*, *going to* | 20 | 73 |
| 49 Logic games | past simple, past continuous | 20 | 74 |
| 50 Alibi | past simple | 20 | 75 |
| 51 Barman | past simple, past perfect | 20 | 76 |
| 52 Mysteries | *can't* and *must* for deductions | 15 | 77 |
| 53 Manager's dilemma | first conditional | 30 | 78 |
| 54 Enigmas | second conditional | 20 | 79 |

| | |
|---|---|
| Introduction | 4 |
| Teacher's notes | 6 |

# Introduction

*Mind Twisters, Puzzles and Games* is a selection of 54 activities based on authentic materials. In fact, nearly all the games, puzzles, jokes and riddles are ones that kids in Britain and the US love to do themselves. These materials have been adapted for your students, to make for amusing and engaging activities through which they will learn and revise their English, and have fun at the same time.

## How to use *Mind Twisters, Puzzles & Games*

The games in this book can be used in a variety of ways. Some shorter activities, e.g. of ten minutes duration, are ideal as warmers at the start of a lesson or time fillers at the end. Other longer activities can be used as the basis for a whole lesson to recycle and practise a recently taught language point.

Within each activity there are generally two or more exercises. Most exercises are linked to each other sequentially, and often one exercise is in preparation for the next. Consequently, you should always check your students' answers to one exercise before proceeding to the next.

The overall activities are *not* designed to present grammar points for the first time but to practise them. So make sure you revise any relevant grammar items beforehand. We have tried to cover a broad range of grammar items typically taught in a student's first three years of English.

This is a photocopiable book, but you don't always need to make photocopies; in many cases you can simply copy the information onto the board.

At the top of each activity there is an indication of the language point(s), the time to allow for the activity, and the level.

**Language point:** This highlights whether particular grammar items or language points are given practice in an activity. *Note*: not all the activities cover a specific grammar point.

**Time:** The clock at the top of each activity indicates the minimum time that activity will take. However, the actual time will very much depend on your class, how much they get into the activity, and how talkative they are. In any case, you should give students a time limit for each individual exercise (particularly for those that require some logical thinking and are not simply based on reading or grammar).

**Level:** This generally corresponds to the vocabulary or grammar that most students who have studied for a particular length of time can be expected to have covered:

  3 to 12 months

  1 to 2 years

  2 to 3 years or more

However, students of higher levels above can also do activities of lower levels. For example, level 3 students can also use level 1 activities. In fact, nearly all the activities can also be used successfully by even more advanced students (i.e. with 4 to 8 years of English) – they make great time fillers.

**Activity titles:** The activity titles give you a rough idea of what vocabulary field you can expect and/or the type of activity (puzzle, riddle, joke, mystery story).

### Vocabulary

Because these are authentic materials, occasionally the vocabulary may seem quite hard. Where possible, such vocabulary items have been illustrated. In any case, more challenging vocabulary and grammar items are a good opportunity to get students to deduce what the meaning might be. They can make such deductions using their native language. Alternatively, encourage students to use a bilingual dictionary. To help you decide which vocabulary items need to be pre-taught, we have included a section on the teacher's pages called 'difficult vocabulary'. The words listed are those found on the students' pages which we think students at this level may not be familiar with, and which are essential to understanding a rubric or which are not illustrated in the cartoons or pictures.

### Skills

This book is designed to encourage students to practise their oral skills in a fun and non-stressful context so, in one way or another, every activity requires students to speak. What students say to each other is actually very important in helping to resolve the problems/games/puzzles, so they will be more motivated than usual to listen to their classmates and to you too! In order to understand how an exercise works, students need to read brief rubrics and longer brainteasers or stories. In some activities a limited amount of writing is also required.

### Instructions

The instructions on the students' pages are designed to be clear. However, our advice would be always to give instructions in the language of your students as they are of vital importance for the success of these exercises.

### Keys

Since one exercise leads into another, give the key (solution) to one exercise before beginning the next. The answers for all exercises are given in the corresponding teacher's notes. However in some cases the answers are visual. These are all on pages 18–21 and can be photocopied and handed out to students.

### Pair and group work

Most of the activities are designed to be done with students working together either in pairs or in groups. Where necessary, the instructions to the exercises on the teacher's pages indicate how many people should be in a group. If your class is not easily divided into, for instance, groups of four, you may decide to have a group of five or six, or two groups of three, and divide up any materials as appropriate.

### A note on lateral-thinking games

Activities 21, 29, 40, 42, 43, 47, 50, 51, 52 and 53 are adaptations of traditional lateral-thinking games. In such games the 'teacher' gives the 'students' a situation. For example, *Anthony and Cleopatra are lying dead in a room, with bits of broken glass around them and a small pool of water.* (Activity 42). The idea is that the 'students' have to ask the 'teacher' a lot of 'yes / no' questions until they discover how Anthony and Cleopatra died. The games are called 'lateral-thinking' because a normal logical approach isn't necessarily the quickest or most effective way to reach the answer. In fact, Anthony and Cleopatra are not humans at all but goldfish! (See key on page 14.)

Typical questions (with related 'yes / no' answers) include:
*Did someone poison them? (no)*
*Did they kill each other? (no)*
*Did someone kill them? (no, not exactly)*

*Is the glass relevant? (yes)*
*Was the glass from a vase? (no)*
*Was it from a bowl? (yes)*
*Did the bowl have water in it? (yes)*
*Did it have anything else in it? (yes)*

*Were they the real Anthony and Cleopatra from history? (no)*

*Is it important that their names are Anthony and Cleopatra? (no)*
*Were they human beings? (no)*
*Were they animals? (yes)*
*Were they fish? (yes)*
*Were they in the bowl? (yes)*
*So something knocked the bowl over? (yes)*
*Was it a cat that had come through the window? (yes)*

What the above groups of questions highlight is that when one line of questioning is apparently exhausted or seems to be getting nowhere, students need to think of another possible approach. So rather than thinking in only one direction, students have to think 'laterally'. In addition, the questions highlight that a variety of tenses can in fact be used / revised – in particular, the present simple, past simple and past perfect.

Be aware that:

- students may blurt out questions in their own native language as they will be keen to get the solution. The way to deal with this is to write the question in the native language on the board, and get the student concerned (or other students) to translate it.

- some students may already know the answer. In this case, form groups with one person who already knows the answer plus three or four (or however many is necessary) who don't know the answer. So instead of students asking you the questions, they ask the student who already knows the answer. You will need to monitor the groups closely to check they are actually doing the exercise in English!

This traditional way of doing these games is the best if you have a group of students who are willing to ask a lot of questions (and it is indeed the most successful way we know of to practise the interrogative form in English, as students are motivated to ask questions to get the solution). The more of these games students do, the quicker and the better they will get at them – and we guarantee that the vast majority of students will love them.

However we have given an alternative presentation, which is less demanding of the students (e.g. by providing the questions students need, by giving them visual clues). We suggest you try the approach given in this book first, and then move on to the traditional approach with any other lateral-thinking games you may find (there are over a hundred on various websites).

*Anna Southern and Adrian Wallwork*

# Teacher's Notes

## 1 Classroom

**1 Individual work**

**Difficult vocabulary:** rhyme

Students do the exercise alone. Then choose particular students to read out the whole row to check their pronunciation.

**Key:** a) Q, b) J, c) O, d) R, e) V

**2 Class work**

**Difficult vocabulary:** aloud

**3 Individual work**

**4 Individual work**

You might want to suggest some lexical sets. Just give students one or two examples in each category, the others they can think of for themselves. Examples:

**home**: kitchen, sitting room

**sport**: football, skiing

**family members**: brother, aunt

**colours**: black, blue

**numbers**: five, thirteen

## 2 Countries

**1 Group work**

**Key:** b) Japan, c) Greece, d) Poland, e) Germany, f) Spain

**2 Individual work**

**Key:** b) Japanese, c) Greek, d) Polish, e) German, f) Spanish

**3 Individual work then pair work**

It doesn't matter how bad students are at drawing; in fact the worse they are, the more fun they are likely to have with this exercise. If some students have difficulty thinking of countries to draw, suggest: Italy, Australia, Argentina, India, Great Britain.

**4 Individual work then pair work**

**Difficult vocabulary:** dangerous, population

With good groups they can ask each other questions, e.g.

Student A: What countries do you want to visit?

Student B: I want to visit ….

**Extension**

Students can write down the nationalities / languages of the countries chosen in Exercise 3.

## 3 The time

**1 Individual and pair work**

Once students have done the exercise, they can ask each other the questions, e.g.

Question: Where are you usually at five o'clock?

Answer: I'm in bed.

**2 Individual or pair work**

**Difficult vocabulary:** reflect, mirror

**Key:** b) a quarter past nine *or* nine fifteen, c) five to nine *or* eight fifty-five, d) six o'clock, e) ten past five *or* five ten, f) twenty five past four *or* four twenty-five, g) a quarter to two *or* one forty-five

**3 Group work**

**Difficult vocabulary:** solve, brainteaser, take, strike *(v)*, how long

This exercise requires simple maths. Allow no more than five minutes to solve it and then explain the solution on the board.

**Key:** 66 seconds. Between the first and sixth strokes, there are five intervals of time, and it takes 30 seconds to cover those five intervals. This means that the interval between two consecutive strokes is six seconds. Between the first stroke and the twelfth, there are 11 intervals. Therefore it takes the clock 66 seconds.

## 4 Colours

**Equipment**: coloured pens for all students

**1 Pair work**

**Difficult vocabulary:** least

If you are teaching a higher-level class, choose one or two items to discuss as a whole class, getting students to give reasons for their choices.

**2 Individual work**

**Difficult vocabulary:** row

If students don't have coloured pens, skip this and move on to Exercise 3.

**3 Individual work**

Make it competitive by seeing who can do it the fastest.

**Key:** There are two possible solutions. The Xs should *not* go in the

1) red, blue and pink boxes

2) brown, blue and purple boxes

See page 18.

## 5 The calendar

**1 Individual or pair work**

When they have finished, they can ask each other the final three questions, e.g. When is your birthday?

**Key:** b) May, c) January, June, July, d) August, e) September, f) March, April, g) December, h) October, November

## 2 Class work

**Difficult vocabulary**: brainteaser, probability

This a famous mathemetical problem; we assure you that the answer given is correct however improbable it may seem. Consult the maths teacher in your school! Or look at this website:
http://www.wiskit.com/marilyn/birthdays.html

Find out from the class if any two people do have the same birthday, or if their best friends or mothers have the same birthdays. Hopefully, you will be able to prove the statistics!

**Key**: b in both cases

## 6 Spot the difference

**Preparation**: this activity is on two pages – one page for each Student A and one for each Student B. Tip: make it easy to see if all the students have the right pages by copying A and B onto different coloured paper.

**Pair work**

**Difficult vocabulary**: similar, difference

Set a time limit and see which pair can find the most differences in the allocated time – without, of course, showing each other their picture. Make sure they ask questions, rather than simply describing their picture.

**Key**: differences (A is first in each of the following): clock 10.50 / 11.10: round table / square table; three people at table / two people; they are eating / not eating but talking; four chairs around table / three chairs; two pictures on wall / one picture; TV on / TV off; daytime / night time; stereo system in room / no stereo system; one window / two windows.

## 7 Habits

**1 Individual work**

Key: 2c, 3d, 4h, 5j, 6b, 7a, 8e, 9g, 10f

**2 Individual work**

**3 Group work**

For this activity students need to know each other quite well.

- Divide the class into groups of five or six.
- Choose one person in each group to be the Questioner.
- Everyone in the group gives their questions to the Questioner.
- All the Questioners leave the classroom.
- Without the Questioners in the room, tell the whole class that they will be asked questions by the Questioners. However, they must answer each question as if they were the person sitting to the right of them.
- If they can't answer for the person sitting to the right of them, they must say 'I don't know'.
- Call the Questioners back into the room and get them to return to their groups.
- Tell the Questioners that they must discover the rule of the game.
- Questioners now begin to ask the questions – they must ask one student a question, and then move on to another student.
- Tell Questioners that when they think they know the rule, they should put their hand up.

Students will probably love playing this game. So here are some alternatives for future lessons:

The first person who is asked a question says 'I don't know'. Then everyone else answers the previous question (i.e. Student 1 says 'I don't know'; Student 2 then answers as if he/she were Student 1).

Students answer the questions as if they were the Questioner.

Students answer the questions as if they were the Teacher.

Students answer the questions as if they were another person in the class who is not in their group.

## 8 The human face

**1 Individual work**

Key: 2a, 3d, 4e, 5b

**2 Group work**

**Difficult vocabulary**: picture

If students see different women, they should try to explain to each other how to see the other woman, e.g. 'nose' or 'this is her nose' or 'this is the old woman's nose'.

**3 Pair work**

Key: see page 18

**4 Individual work**

**Difficult vocabulary**: mean (v), trendy, friendly, extrovert, traditional, wise, introvert, genius

## 9 Rooms

**1 Individual work**

**Difficult vocabulary**: store, keep

Key: 2a, 3f, 4g, 5b, 6e, 7d

**2 Individual work**

**Difficult vocabulary**: plan (n)

Tell students just to draw a very simple diagram. If their house is enormous, they should just draw some, not all, of the rooms. If their flat is very small, they can add some extra rooms.

**3 Group work**

Put students in groups of any size. Imagining a group of three, students should proceed as follows:

**3a)** Student A passes his / her drawing to Student B, Student B to Student C, and Student C to Student A. All three students now write a description of the drawing they have in front of them.

**3b)** Student A passes his / her description to Student B, Student B to Student C, and Student C to Student A. All three students now do a drawing based on the description they have in front of them.

**3c)** Students now compare the drawings they did in 3b with the original drawings from Exercise 2. In theory the two drawings should be the same, but inevitably they will be different – with more advanced groups, this could be a discussion point.

**4 Individual work**

Key: see page 18

## 10 Picture puzzles

**Difficult vocabulary**: **1** alternately; **2** straight; **3** upside-down

**Pair work**

Give students a ten-minute time limit to solve as many of the problems as possible.

With more advanced students, divide into groups of three. Give each student one problem with the related key, plus the other two problems. Their task is to enable the other two students to do the problem for which they have the key by providing them with instructions.

Key: see page 19

## 11 Smileys

**1 Individual work**

Before beginning the exercise, draw this smiley :-) on the board. Ask if anyone knows what it is (a symbol used in emails and chatlines* to denote that you are joking – it represents someone smiling). As with all western smileys, it can be best appreciated by being viewed vertically (Japanese smileys are horizontal).

Key: b7, c5, d6, e1, f8, g3, h10, i4, j9

**2 Pair work**

Encourage the students to make comparisons, e.g. 'Number 2 *looks like* a clown'.

Key: 2a, 3g, 4d, 5e, 6h, 7c, 8j, 9f, 10b

*See note about chatlines on page 11.

## 12 Quantities

**1 Individual work**

**Difficult vocabulary**: earth, belly

Key:
**1** a+b) not heavy enough, c) correct
**2** a) not tall enough, b) correct, c) too tall
**3** a) correct, b+c) too long
**4** a) not old enough, b) correct, c) too old
**5** a) correct, b+c) too old

**2 Individual work**

Key: 2 too many people, 3 too many bags, 4 not enough chicken/food, 5 not enough money, 6 too much water

## 13 Geography

**1 Individual work**

**Difficult vocabulary**: shallow, border, building, populated, crime rate

Key: a) longer, b) deeper, c) lower, d) smaller, e) longer, f) younger, g) taller, h) more, i) further from, j) worse

**2 Individual work then pair work**

**Difficult vocabulary**: continent, calorie consumption, producer, hemisphere

Key:
b) strongest F
c) most F (it's Africa)
d) greatest / highest T (but there are more native Chinese speakers than native English speakers)
e) fewest T
f) longest T
g) highest / biggest / greatest T
h) biggest T (it's not in the top 10 but is in the top 20)
i) richest F (Australia is)
j) hardest F

## 14 Food and drink

**Preparation**: see note at the top of Activity 6 Spot the difference.

When a student has finished, they can then check with their picture to see how much they have remembered.

## 15 Crazy conundrums

**Difficult vocabulary**: crazy, conundrum

**1 Individual work**

Key: b5, c1, d3, e6, f4

**2 Individual work**

**Difficult vocabulary**: (a) mouse/mice, mirror; (b) get wet; (c) wear, mask, blackout, street light, cross *(v)*, headlights, turn *(v)*, hit *(v)*, driver

With very low level groups only do (a).

Key: (a) 2 in front of, 3 behind, 4 in front of, 5 behind; (b) 6 next to, 7 under; (c) 8 at, 9 towards

**3 Group work**

Set a suitable time limit.

Key: (a) The third mouse is a liar! (b) It is not raining! (c) It was during the day!

## 16 Family members

**1 Individual work then whole class**

Key: Margaret: grandmother; Arthur: grandfather; Stephen: father; Anna: daughter; Charles: son

### 2 Individual work then whole class

**Key**: in the male section: brother, nephew, son, uncle; in the middle section (i.e. either male or female): baby, children, cousin; in the female section: aunt, daughter, niece, sister

### 3 Group work

**Difficult vocabulary**: brainteaser; (b) three times, twice; (c) sure, that's right; (d) related; (e) point *(v)*

Set a time limit.

**Key**:
a) grandmother, mother, daughter
b) 12
c) There are two men and each marries the mother of the other man. They both have one son from this marriage. So each of the sons will be both uncle and nephew of the other. (Students may also come up with other valid solutions.)
d) Cristina is Emma's mother.
e) The boy is the sister's son.
f) Four. The father and mother are brother and sister, one having one son, and the other a daughter.

## 17 Jail break

**Individual work**

**Key**: 2 must, 3 cannot, 4 can, 5 cannot, 6 must

See page 19

## 18 Coin game

**Individual work**

**Difficult vocabulary**: aim, move

**Key**: see page 20

## 19 Work it out

### 1 Pair or group work

**Difficult vocabulary**: (students will need to know these words) (a) lift, stuck, bow tie; (b) panda, climb *(v)*; (c) pig, fog; (d) fry; (e) rowing boat

If the students have no ideas, you could give them the answers in the wrong order and ask them to match the pictures to the explanations.

**Key**:
a) a waiter's bow tie stuck in a lift
b) a panda climbing a tree
c) a pig in the fog
d) a Mexican man frying an egg
e) a rowing boat seen from above

### 2 Pair or group work

**Difficult vocabulary**: (a) cock, lay; (b) cherry, ice; (c) bull

**Key**:
a) Cocks of course don't lay eggs.
b) If the river has ice on it, it must be winter, so there won't be cherries on the tree.
c) Bulls don't produce milk.
d) There are in fact four crosses in the picture; the biggest one is the one that divides the four pictures.

## 20 Numbers

### 1 Pair or group work

**Difficult vocabulary**: password

Set a five-minute deadline.

**Key**: eight. The code is in the number of letters in each number, e.g. o-n-e has three letters so you say 'three'.

### 2 Individual work

**Difficult vocabulary**: grid, add up to

**Key**: see page 20

## 21 School bus

**Note**: Read page 5 of the Introduction for ideas on how to conduct and exploit lateral-thinking games.

### 1 Individual work

**Difficult vocabulary**: get off, ride

At this point students do not attempt to answer the question.

### 2 Individual work

**Difficult vocabulary**: on time

Make sure students know that *some* is used in affirmative sentences and *any* in negative sentences. N.B. This exercise does not deal with *some* and *any* in interrogative sentences.

**Key**: b) something, c) any, d) any, e) any, f) any, g) anyone, h) some, i) any

### 3 Group work

**Difficult vocabulary**: relevant

**Key**: f) She gets off at the second stop, and walks downhill to school. If she wanted to do some exercise, she would get off at the first stop and walk uphill. However, students may come up with other rational explanations.

## 22 Guess the object

### 1 Pair or group work

**Difficult vocabulary**: object (n)

Set a five-minute time limit.

**Key**: 1 a bicycle, 2 (the top of) a bottle, 3 a chair, 4 (a bar of) chocolate, 5 an ear, 6 a fish, 7 (the lock on) a suitcase, 8 a shoe, 9 a plane

### 2 Group work

**Difficult vocabulary**: discover

Put students in groups of three to six. The person who gets the answer then thinks of another object. Students should make sure that everyone in their group has an opportunity to think of an object.

## Extension

Group work. In turn, and without the others looking, each student puts an object into a bag (bags made of some kind of textile are best – plastic and paper bags tend to get destroyed quite easily, particularly if the objects are spiky). There should only be one object in the bag at a time. The others in the group then feel the bag and decide what is inside. This is then repeated with another object from another student.

## 23 Experiences

**1 Individual work**

**Difficult vocabulary**: speed, travel, meal, delicious

**Key**: a) biggest, b) best, c) happiest, d) furthest, e) most terrifying, f) highest, g) fastest, h) most expensive, i) most delicious j) worst

**2 Individual work**

**3 Pair work**

**4 Individual then pair work**

**Difficult vocabulary**: boring, ridiculous

The questions needn't contain the present perfect if you are only interested in practice of superlatives.

## 24 High numbers

**Preparation**: see note at the top of Activity 6 Spot the difference.

**1 Whole class**

**Difficult vocabulary**: guess, lifetime

Use this activity to revise high numbers in preparation for Exercise 2.

**Note**: These statistics were compiled from a variety of books and websites, and supposedly refer to the average American or Briton. Clearly, as with all statistics, they are open to interpretation and it is not known how many people took part in any associated surveys or how the researchers arrived at their conclusions. In any case, they are simply meant to be a fun way of practising large numbers. If your students contest them, suggest that they do their own Internet searches to prove you wrong!

**Key**: 1d, 2d, 3c, 4c

**2 Pair work**

**Difficult vocabulary**: blink, trillion, flush

Make sure students understand they have different bits of information that they are going to exchange with each other.

**Key**: we blink 682 million times; we eat 7,800 loaves of bread; we flush the toilet 109,200 times; we lose 136 kilogrammes of skin; we spend 25 years sleeping; we take 13,650 baths or showers; we use 2,574 toilet rolls; we walk 240,000 kilometres; we watch 12 years of TV; we wear 675 pairs of underpants.

## 25 Number games

**Preparation**: see note at the top of Activity 6 Spot the difference.

Pre-teach *add, subtract, multiply, double* and *divide by*, writing their symbols on the board.

Now try this game on your students.

Tell the class to think of a number; each student can choose their own number. Then give them the following directions. An example is given in the right-hand column:

| | |
|---|---|
| Think of a number – don't tell me what it is | 6 |
| Double the number | 6 x 2 = 12 |
| Add 4 | 12 + 4 = 16 |
| Divide by 2 | 16 / 2 = 8 |
| Add 13 | 8 + 13 = 21 |

Then choose a student and ask him / her for the result (21 in the example above). Subtract 15 from their answer and give them the result (6 in the example). This works with whatever number a student chooses – the answer is always the number first thought of (but practise doing it with family members first!).

For the games on the students' pages, put students into pairs.

**1 Individual work**

Tell students that they are going to play a similar mathematical game on their partner. The example should help them to decide where to insert the verbs and also how the game functions. When students have completed the exercise, write the answers on the board as follows. It doesn't matter if they see one another's answers.

Student A: b) don't tell, c) subtract, d) double, e) add, f) add, g) divide

Student B: b) don't tell, c) add, d) multiply, e) subtract, f) divide, g) subtract

**2 Pair work**

**3 Pair work**

## 26 Farmer's dilemma

**1 Individual work**

**Difficult vocabulary**: need, attack

**2 Group work**

Encourage students to work as a team in resolving the problem.

**Key**: the farmer first takes over the sheep and leaves it. He then returns, fetches the dog, leaves the dog, and takes back the sheep. He leaves the sheep and takes over the hay. He leaves the hay with the dog. He then returns and brings over the sheep. (Alternatively, he takes the hay on the second trip.)

**3 Individual work**

This exercise highlights that the *if*-clause can come in the first or second half of the sentence.

**4 Pair work**

## 27 School jokes

**Individual work**

**Difficult vocabulary**: (b) improve, case; (c) quiet; (d) boring, shut something or someone up (e) report

Ask the whole class which jokes they think are the funniest and check that everyone has actually understood them.

**Key**: 2b, 3d, 4a, 5f, 6e

b) can, c) can't, d) can, e) can't, f) Can

## 28 Teacher jokes

**1 Individual work**

**Difficult vocabulary**: (b) chew; (c) copy, check *(v)*; (d) keep doing something; (f) manage

**Key**: b) Are you chewing, c) are you copying, am just checking d) do you call, e) like, f) do you manage, arrive

**2 Pair work**

**Difficult vocabulary**: joke, riddle, at this very moment

As an alternative, you can put the phrases on separate pieces of paper. Then follow this procedure:

- Divide class into groups of three.
- Give two slips of paper to each person in the group.
- In turn, each person reads one slip of paper.
- Without showing one another their slips of paper, they try and work out what the order is.
- If this proves too difficult, they can put the slips of paper on a desk, and then order them together.

**Key**: b, e;   c, h, g, d

## 29 Lift mystery

**Warning!** This game is perhaps best not played if you have any members of the class who have an inferiority complex about their height or are frequently teased about it.

**Note:** Read page 5 of the Introduction for ideas on how to conduct and exploit lateral-thinking games.

**1 Individual work**

Note. As students read, check to see if anyone already knows the story (it's a very famous one), but make sure they don't tell anyone the solution.

**2 Individual work**

**Difficult vocabulary**: do some exercise, superstitious, vertigo, claustrophobia, relevant, alone

These are the typical questions people ask when trying to solve this puzzle. They are put here so that weaker students have a chance to ask questions. With more advanced groups, get students to invent their own questions without looking at the ones on their sheet.

**3 Group work**

Divide the class into groups and tell one student in each group the solution (or use the students who already know the game). Then the other members of the group ask questions until they find the solution.

Alternatively, the whole class can ask you the questions.

**Key**:
Does he know someone on the 13th floor? No.
Does he want to do some exercise? No.
Is he superstitious? No.
Does he suffer from vertigo or claustrophobia? No.
Does the lift go from the 13th floor to the 20th floor? Yes.
Is it relevant that he works in a bank? No.
Does he always get out of the lift at the 13th floor? No.
If he's not alone in the lift, does he get out at the 13th floor? No.
Does he have a particular problem? Yes.
Answer: Joe is too small to reach the 20 button in the lift. Clearly, if he is with someone else in the lift who is going to his floor, he will be able to get out at the 20th floor.

## 30 Chatline acronyms

**Difficult vocabulary**: acronym

Remind students of the potential dangers of using chatlines and chatrooms – tell them they should never arrange to meet someone without their parents' permission and never give out phone numbers or addresses.

**1 Whole class**

**2 Whole class**

Before doing the exercise, ask students if they recognise the three acronyms below (each letter stands for one word).

lol = (I am) laughing out loud

wayd = what are you doing?

paw = (my) parents are watching

N.B. in chatline acronyms auxiliary verbs (*am, have, do, did*, etc), articles (*the, a*) and possessive pronouns (*my, your*, etc) are usually omitted.

**Key**: 2f, 3d, 4a, 5g, 6e, 7c, 8b

**3 Individual work**

**Key**:
| | |
|---|---|
| 2 crbt | h) crying real big tears |
| 3 hhoj | e) ha ha only joking |
| 4 lho | f) laughing head off |
| 5 pal | b) parents are listening |
| 6 rotfl | a) rolling on the floor laughing |
| 7 sete | g) smiling ear to ear |
| 8 toy | c) thinking of you |

## 31 Riddles

**1 Class work**

**Difficult vocabulary**: riddle, as long as

**Key**: fire

**2 Individual work**

**Difficult vocabulary**: touch, hidden, hold, hole, take away

**Key**: b) use, c) comes, d) is, e) holds, f) has, g) becomes, h) spell, i) moves, j) has

**3 Pair or group work**

**Key**: a) the sun (1), b) your name (4), c) the letter M (5), d) an iceberg (7), e) a sponge (3) f) a box of matches (2), g) a hole (6), h) 'incorrectly' (8), i) a mirror (9), j) half a centipede (10)

## 32 Giving directions

**1 Individual work then group work**

**Difficult vocabulary**: travel, underground, preference, both, platform

Students read the text individually, then in groups they try and resolve the problem (it is one of simple mathematics).

**Key**: imagine that the train for the Central Train Station leaves at 12.00, 12.10, 12.20, 12.30, etc. If the train for the Cathedral leaves one minute later at 12.01, 12.11, etc. then the only time Julia would be able to catch the Cathedral train would be in the interval just after 12.00 and before 12.01. Whereas if she arrives after 12.01 there is a nine-minute interval in which she can catch the train for the Central Train Station.

**2 Pair work**

**Difficult vocabulary**: stop (n), get off/on

## 33 Ask the teacher

**Warning!** In this exercise, your students will be asking you personal questions. Make sure you think all the questions are acceptable. If you think some are too personal, then you can delete them with whitener. In any case, remember you don't necessarily have to be truthful if that will avoid embarrassment or simply make the lesson more interesting.

**1 Individual work**

**Key**: b) break broke broken, c) do did done, d) drive drove driven, e) fall fell fallen, f) have had had, g) lose lost lost, h) meet met met, i) see saw seen, j) take took taken

**2 Pair work**

**Difficult vocabulary**: scout, girl guide (female scout), ghost, speed limit, expensive

The idea is to practise the difference between the past simple and the present perfect. In this context, i.e. in relation to you the teacher, the past simple is used for an action that took place in some defined period of your past, e.g. when you were a child or were at school / university. The present perfect is used for an experience you have had at some unspecified point in your life and which could take place again now or in the future.

**3 Pair work**

**Difficult vocabulary**: definitely not

**4 Class work**

- You can either go around the class or get students to ask questions at random.
- Tell students they are only allowed to ask one question. Remember that they will have two of their own questions to ask.
- With a good group, encourage them to ask follow-up questions. Example:

  Student: Have you ever met anyone famous?
  You: Yes.
  Student: Who have you met?
  You: I once met Britney Spears.
  Student: Where did you meet her?

## 34 Visual game

**1 Pair work**

**Difficult vocabulary**: a) match, coin

The idea of this exercise is to add a new element to the task by getting students to analyse how potentially difficult the problems are. This makes the problems more interesting to solve as they turn out to be more or less difficult than imagined.

**2 Pair work**

**Key**: see page 21

## 35 Horse race

**1 Individual work**

**Difficult vocabulary**: ride (v)

Make sure students understand that some of the parts are correct and others contain mistakes.

**Key**: a) become becAme becOme, b) chOOse chose chosen, c) cost COST COST, d) fall fELL fALLEN, e) find FOUND FOUND, j) teach tAUGHT tAUGHT

**2 Individual work**

**Difficult vocabulary**: horse race, make up (invent), rules, cross (v), get on / off, gallop

N.B. Only *ride* from Exercise 1 appears in this exercise, since it is not a common irregular verb.

**Key**: 2 rode, 3 began, 4 got, 5 came, 6 said, 7 got, 8 won

**3 Group work**

Set a three-minute time limit.

If they need a clue, tell students that when the girlfriend gives them the solution, they are not on their horses. Then the text says: they both got on *a* horse (not *their* horses).

**Key**: she said: 'Change horses'. Remember the rule was the horse (not the jockey) that crosses the line last wins, so if they change horses and win as jockeys, then their horse, ridden by the other jockey, will win the race.

## 36 Maths

**1 Individual work**

**Difficult vocabulary**: a) mouse / mice; b) blow *(v)*, smoke; c) encyclopaedia, numerical, cover, volume, thick, travel; d) get ready, be about to, sock, drawer; e) haystack; f) tunnel

**Key**: b) is going, is blowing, c) starts, stops, d) will / do, get,
e) puts, will, f) will, is

**2 Pair or group work**

This 'test' actually requires more logical (or illogical!) thinking than mathematical ability, but don't tell students this as part of the fun is realising that you have been approaching the exercise in completely the wrong way.

- Tell students to do as many of the questions as they can in 15 minutes.
- Possibly give a prize to the group who manages to answer the most questions within 15 minutes.
- Give the answers. The answer to c) you will need to explain on the board.

**Key**:
a) an hour and a half
b) There won't be any smoke because the train is electric!
c) 0.6 cm – the thickness of the two covers. In fact, if you put two books together and see where the first begins and the second ends, you will see that the two closest covers to these points are adjacent to each other.
d) three
e) one
f) two minutes: it takes one minute for the train to go into the tunnel and another minute for the whole train to be out the other side.

## 37 Silly maths

**Pair work**

**Difficult vocabulary**: a) tied, rope, hay; b) sack, corn; c) ark; d) butcher, weigh; e) dirt, hole, ground; g) envelope, at random

Make the activity competitive by giving a time limit of ten minutes. The pair that gets the most correct answers in that time wins.

**Key**
a) The rope is only tied to the horse, not to anything else.
b) Your friend, because three sacks of corn weigh more than simply four (empty) sacks.
c) It was Noah's ark not Moses'.
d) He weighed meat.
e) It's a hole so there's no dirt in it.
f) Josh.
g) Nil – if four are correct, then all five must be.
h) 21. This is the only one that requires a calculation. Imagine there are seven people called A, B, C, D, E, F and G. A will shake hands with B-G (six handshakes), B with C-F (five, A and B have already shaken hands ), C with D-G (four), D with E-G (three), E with F and G (two), and F with G (one). 6+5+4+3+2+1 = 21.

## 38 Text messaging

**1 Pair work**

**Difficult vocabulary**: mobile phone, maniac, features, technophobe, cool guy

Students discuss their answers as they complete the quiz.

**2 Individual work**

**Key**: a) 4, b) 1, c) 3, d) 2

**3 Group work**

**Key**: a) how are you?, b) see you later today, c) are you free tonight?, d) wait for me at the cinema

**Extension**

Students could write some of their own text messages.

## 39 Loch Ness Monster

**1 Individual work**

**Difficult vocabulary**: photographic equipment, camera, smash, leak, oil slick

**Key**: 2 was sent, 3 put, 4 spent, 5 found, 6 was smashed, 7 doubled, 8 became, 9 was covered

**2 Group work**

**Key**: one more day (if it doubles every day, then the next day it will be covered completely).

## 40 Night watchman

**Note:** Read page 5 of the Introduction for ideas on how to conduct and exploit lateral-thinking games.

**1 Individual work**

**Difficult vocabulary**: night watchman, fire *(v)*, temperature

**Key**: 2a, 3e, 4f, 5d, 6g, 7c

**2 Pair work**

**Key**: he was sleeping instead of working (i.e. he shouldn't have been sleeping during work time).

## 41 Beastly brainteasers

**Difficult vocabulary**: beastly, brainteasers

**1 Pair work**

**Difficult vocabulary**: a) chain, link *(v/n)*, jeweller, manage; c) coin, edge; d) triangle

The idea of this exercise is to add a new element to the task by getting students to analyse how potentially difficult the problems are. This makes the problems more interesting to solve as they turn out to be more or less difficult than imagined.

**2 Pair work**

**Key**:
a) If you undo all the links in one of the chains (four

operations), you can then use these opened links to join the other five chains together (another four operations).
b) see page 21
c) see page 21
d) see page 21

## 42 Detectives

**Note:** Read page 5 of the Introduction for ideas on how to conduct and exploit lateral-thinking games.

**1 Group work**

**Difficult vocabulary**: detective, relevant, witness

Pre-teach 'witness' (i.e. someone who is at the scene of a crime and sees what happens).

Note. Check to see if anyone already knows the story, but make sure they don't tell anyone the solution.

**2 Class work**

If no one already knows the solution, students ask you their questions. If one or more students do already know the solution, then form groups in which one person in each group knows the answer.

**Key**: Anthony and Cleopatra were two gold fish, not the famous historical figures. A cat had come in the room through a window and knocked the fish bowl onto the floor. The glass from the bowl broke into many pieces and obviously the fish died.

## 43 Hotel mystery

**Note:** Read page 5 of the Introduction for ideas on how to conduct and exploit lateral-thinking games.

**Preparation**: photocopy the picture story, bearing in mind that each photocopy will be enough for five students. Cut the story up into its five parts. Paste each onto a card (you will then be able to re-use the game in other lessons).

**Group work**

- Put students into groups of five.
- Give each student in the group one of the five pictures.*
- Tell students not to show their picture to anyone else.
- In turn, students must describe what is in their picture. They can ask each other questions to clarify.
- When they have all described their pictures, they should try and decide the most logical order for the pictures.
- Finally, they should answer the following question, which you can write on the board: 'Why do you think the woman made the phone call?'

* If you have four students left over, then give one of them two pictures; with three students, give two of them two pictures or make two groups of four with one person in each group having two pictures. If you have two students left over, make three groups of four with one person in each group having two pictures.

**Key**:

A man is snoring in his hotel bed.

A woman in the next room is trying to get to sleep.

She gets up, goes to the telephone and dials a number.

She waits for the man to answer and immediately puts the phone down.

She goes back to bed and goes to sleep.

**Solution**: The person she rings was snoring, so by phoning she wakes him up and thus can go back to sleep herself.

**Extension**

Students could write the story out in full, using the past simple and past continuous.

## 44 Doctor jokes

**1 Individual work**

**Difficult vocabulary**: joke, yo-yo, keep doing something, ignore

Check answers with the whole class and make sure they understand the jokes!

Key: 2a, 3e, 4c, 5b

**2 Pair work**

**Difficult vocabulary**: 1 bite (v); 2 wonder, bored, shut up; 3 what seems to be the trouble; 5 invisible, optician; 6 tell the truth

The answers given in the key are the 'correct' ones, but students may think of reasons for finding the other answers funny.

Key: 2a, 3a, 4b, 5a, 6b

**3 Pair work**

**Difficult vocabulary**: muddled up, keep doing something, see double, lift, strength, pill, couch, get something off

Key: 2 b, f, k; 3 c, e, j; 4 d, h, i

## 45 Crack the code

**Difficult vocabulary**: crack, code

**1 Individual work**

**Difficult vocabulary**: chatline, cheat (v), ride, prize, poem, crash, stay up, tell lies, travel, hovercraft

This exercise is in preparation for the game in Exercise 2.

Explain that *Do you ever* is for habitual events in the present, and *Have you ever* for past experiences. Divide the class into two groups. Students in Group 1 invent questions using the phrases in the first column, and students in Group 2 using the phrases in the second column.

**2 Group work**

Form new groups with some members from Group 1 and some from Group 2.

In addition, form one other group: the Interviewees.

Tell the Interviewees that the other students will ask them questions. They must reply, for example, 'yes, I have' or 'no, I don't' depending on the last letter in the question. If the last letter is from A-O they must answer 'yes', if the last letter is from P-Z they must answer 'no'. Give them some examples, e. g. 'Have you ever cheated in an exaM?' 'Yes, I have.' 'Do you play any sportS?' 'No, I don't.'

Now put one Interviewee into each of the other groups.

Tell the whole class that in their groups they must ask the Interviewee questions. The Interviewee will answer 'yes' or 'no' on the basis of some code. Their task is to discover what code the interviewee is using.

**Extension**

If there is time, change Interviewees and try one of these alternatives.

Interviewees answer questions on the basis of whether the questioner:

– is a boy ('yes') or girl ('no')

– is wearing glasses ('yes'), is not wearing glasses ('no')

– has brown eyes ('yes'), does not have brown eyes ('no')

There are obviously various other alternatives to the game, which you will be able to invent yourself. It is a game that students will love and can be repeated in several lessons.

## 46 English humour

**1 Pair work**

**Difficult vocabulary**: joke, handwriting, memory, should have been, happen, see into the future, borrow, prove

**Key**: 2a, 3g, 4f, 5e, 6c, 7b

**2 Individual work**

**Key**: a) forgot, b) have changed, c) started, e) did not play, f) did what happen, g) happened

## 47 Shoe mystery

**Note**: Read page 5 of the Introduction for ideas on how to conduct and exploit lateral-thinking games.

**1 Group work and individual work**

Students should discuss the solution together before individually writing the explanation.

**2 Group work**

Students exchange stories with another group and see if they have come up with the same solution. Take a class vote to see which picture they used in the solution. Then give students the 'real' solution. Note, however, that the students' own solutions may be equally good.

**Key**: Picture 3. The woman is the assistant to a circus knife-thrower. Her job is to stand in front of a target as knives are thrown around her. She has bought new shoes that have a slightly higher heel than her normal shoes, so the thrower doesn't get his aim right and hits her.

## 48 School facilities

**Note**: the time this exercise takes and its success very much depend on the level of the group and how communicative they are. Do not attempt it with very reticent classes.

**1 Group work**

**Difficult vocabulary**: governor, exchange trip, pottery, school trip, canteen, playground, heating, air conditioning

Put students in groups of four or five.

Make sure they understand that their budget of €10 will only cover some of the items in the list, since the total value of the list is €20.

Explain the costs are of course only symbolic and that in reality they would be hundreds of thousands of euros.

**2 Group work**

Rearrange the groups so that you have a new group consisting of at least one member of each of the original groups.

Students then explain their choices to each other.

Finally, as a whole class, see if they can agree on how to spend their €10.

## 49 Logic games

**1 Individual work**

**Difficult vocabulary**: a) lie (as in 'not tell the truth'), elder; b) blow, pick up, belong, windy, chances, get back, own (adj)

Note: Make sure students understand the difference between the past simple and the past continuous. In this particular exercise, the past simple is used for a short action or a series of actions. The past continuous is used to describe a long action which was interrupted by a short action.

**Key**:
a) 2 went, 3 was cooking, 4 ran, 5 looked, 6 was listening, 7 knew, 8 were telling, 9 told, 10 knew, 11 was lying, 12 lied, 13 was listening, 14 came

b) 15 was, 16 were walking, 17 blew, 18 was passing, 19 picked, 20 belonged, 21 gave

**2 Pair or group work**

**Key**:
a) It was Anna. Julia told the truth when she denied listening to the CD; Richard told the truth when he said it was one of the girls; Adrian lied when he accused Richard; and Anna told the truth when she said that Adrian was lying.
b) If nine people get their hat back, then the remaining person must get their hat too. So exactly nine is not possible.

## 50 Alibi

**Note:** Read page 5 of the Introduction for ideas on how to conduct and exploit lateral-thinking games.

**1 Individual work**

**Difficult vocabulary:** DJ (disk jockey), alibi

**Key:** 1, 5, 9, 6, 3, 4, 2, 8, 7, 10, 11 or: 1, 5, 9, 6, 4, 2, 8, 3, 7, 10, 11

**2 Pair work**

Set a time limit and then elicit answer from whole class.

**Key:** picture 10 shows that the CD had got stuck and was repeating itself, which happens when a CD is dirty or defective. His alibi was thus blown because the police would know that he wasn't really at work.

This is the complete story.

A DJ wants to kill his wife but needs an alibi. So he goes to the radio station where he works, puts on a CD, slips out to go home, kills his wife, drives back to the radio station and, while driving, turns on the radio to his own programme. He hears the CD repeating itself; he thus knows his alibi has been blown.

**Extension**

Copy the following onto the board. Students write (in the past simple) the story of the DJ, using these words and phrases as prompts:

radio station – programme – puts on a CD – leaves – drives home – goes inside – kills wife – gets back in car – turns on radio – hears ???? – shoots himself

## 51 Barman

**Note:** Read page 5 of the Introduction for ideas on how to conduct and exploit lateral-thinking games.

With more advanced classes, don't give the students the photocopy but just tell them the story. They then have to invent questions of their own to ask you.

**The story:**
A woman goes into a bar and asks for something to drink. The barman takes out a gun and points it at her. She says 'thank you' and leaves.

**1 Individual work**

**Difficult vocabulary:** arrange, shocked, pills, medicine, solve

**Key:** b) had, c) had, d) did, e) were, f) had, g) was, h) did, i) was, j) did, k) did, l) had, m) did

**2 Whole class**

Students ask you the questions. Alternatively, put students in small groups and tell one person in each group the solution. The members of the group then ask questions.

Remind them that they must be yes/no questions, not *wh-* questions.

**Key:** she had hiccups and the fright cured her.
a) yes, probably, but not necessarily
b) perhaps, but it's not very important
c) perhaps, not important
d) yes
e) irrelevant
f) irrelevant
g) yes
h) no
i) good question, no
j) good question, no
k) yes
l) probably
m) yes

## 52 Mysteries

**Note:** Read page 5 of the Introduction for ideas on how to conduct and exploit lateral-thinking games.

**1 Group work**

**Difficult vocabulary:**

1 smoke

2 search party, blood, building, shoot *(v)*, evidence, arrest, murderer

3 stranger, pay in cash, clerk

4 lawyer, grant bail, be allowed

5 suspect *(v)*, leave something behind, evidence

Get students to cover the bottom half of their page, where the solutions are.

Students read the mysteries and try to solve them in their groups. Tell them that if they can't solve them, it doesn't matter. Allow not more than ten minutes to complete Exercise 1.

**2 Group work**

**Difficult vocabulary:** alone, cell, perfume, blind, reveal, toilet seat up

Students try and match the solutions with the mysteries. Because the solutions are so short (i.e. without much explanation) and because there are extra solutions, this activity will involve discussion. Get students to give explanations for their choices.

**Key:**
1 d (She is in prison in a cell, so she can't do anything about it.)
2 g
3 f (Teresa is blind so she won't be able to count out the money. She goes to a bank where she knows the bank clerk will count the money correctly.)
4 i (It is Petra's lawyer who is being held in prison, not Petra herself.)
5 h (Mrs Smith lives alone with Natasha, so the toilet seat would always be down unless a man came into the house.)

**MIND TWISTERS, PUZZLES & GAMES** Teacher's notes

## 53 Manager's dilemma

**Note:** Read page 5 of the Introduction for ideas on how to conduct and exploit lateral-thinking games.

**1 Individual work**

- Tell students to look at the pictures and to try and understand what is going on in each picture.
- Identify any vocabulary problems.
- Now read the story below very slowly and clearly, with long pauses between paragraphs to enable students to find the relevant picture. Make sure the students realise there is one picture per paragraph.
- Read the story again, either more slowly or more quickly depending on how successful students have been in understanding it on the first reading.
- Give them a couple of minutes to make their final decision about the order of the pictures – they can do this in pairs or groups if you wish.

    Alternative with higher level students: only give students the photocopies of the illustrations after they have listened to the story. Then in pairs they can try and work out the correct order.

    **Key**: 1d, 2f, 3a, 4c, 5e, 6b

**2 Group work**

**Key**: Arnie notices that Mr Gold has put two black stones in the bag, but he says nothing. Arnie then picks out one stone from the bag and drops it immediately onto the ground (where there are thousands of white and black stones). He then says 'Sorry, but if we look into the bag and see which stone is left, then we will know which one I dropped.' Clearly, the one in the bag is black, so the other one should have been white.

**3 Individual work**

### The story

A football manager needed 20 million Euros to rebuild his club's football stadium. He went to a rich businessman, Mr Gold, who gave him the money. (pause)

It took six months to rebuild the stadium. But on the first day of the new football season, some hooligans burnt down part of the stadium. (pause)

Mr Gold, who was worried about this situation, immediately telephoned the manager to ask him for the 20 million Euros. But the manager said he didn't have the money. So Mr Gold told the manager to meet him at his office car park and to come with his best player, Arnie Ball. (pause)

The three men met and Mr Gold said, 'If you give me your best player, I will cancel your debt.' The manager replied, 'If I give you Arnie Ball, no one will come to watch my team play.' (pause)

'OK.' said Mr Gold, 'Look at these stones on the ground. They are all black or white. I will pick up two stones, a black one and a white one, and put them into this little bag. If Arnie picks out the black stone from this bag, then you will have to give him to me. But if he picks out the white one, then he will be free and I will cancel your debt.' The manager agreed as he had no choice. (pause)

Mr Gold picked up two stones and put them in his bag, but Arnie noticed that Mr Gold had put two black stones in his bag. How did Arnie resolve the situation?

## 54 Enigmas

**Difficult vocabulary**: enigma

**1 Individual work**

**Difficult vocabulary**: punchline

**Key**: a) 3, b) 5, c) 2, d) 4, e) 1

**2 Group work**

**Difficult vocabulary**: thirst, tell lies (not tell the truth)

Give them a chance to solve it by themselves, then put them into groups or pairs to see if they can work out which is the correct solution.

**Key**: c

## MIND TWISTERS, PUZZLES & GAMES — Visual answers

**4 Colours**

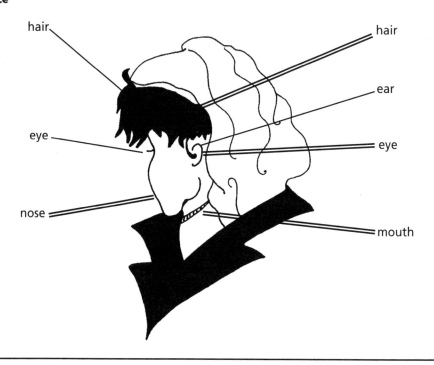

**8 The human face**

**9 Rooms**

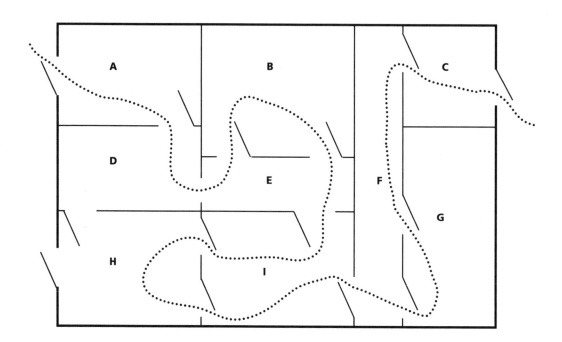

**MIND TWISTERS, PUZZLES & GAMES**  Visual answers

### 10 Picture puzzles

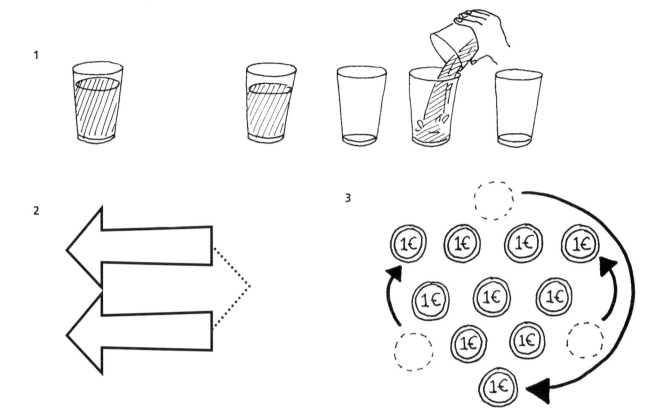

### 17 Jail break

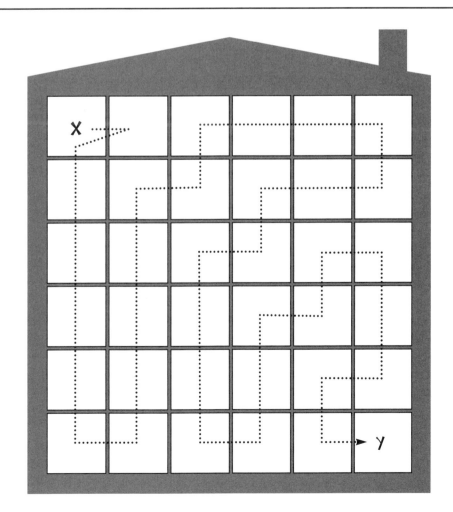

**18 Coin game**

The four moves are:

1 2 3 4 5 6 7 8 9 10

**1)** 2 and 3 to 9 and 10

**2)** 5 and 6 to 2 and 3

**3)** 8 and 9 to 5 and 6

**4)** 1 and 2 to 8 and 9

---

**20 Numbers**

| 4 | 9 | 2 |
|---|---|---|
| 3 | 5 | 7 |
| 8 | 1 | 6 |

**MIND TWISTERS, PUZZLES & GAMES** Visual answers

### 34 Visual game

 a)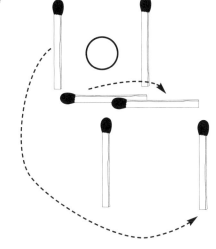

 b)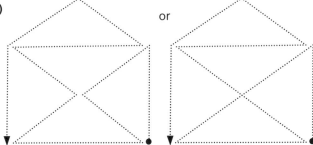

 c)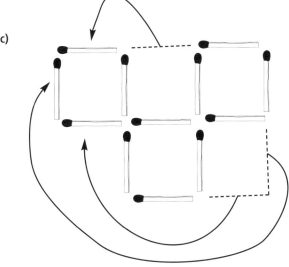

### 41 Beastly brainteasers

 b)   c)  d)

# 1 Classroom

**1** Which letter does not rhyme with the first letter?

Example: E F̲ B D T

a) A H J K Q
b) B C D E G J P T V
c) F L M N O S X
d) I R Y
e) U V Q W

**2** Read aloud the letters in the word circles, starting at the top.

a) E D S K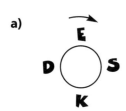
b) N D O W W I
c) U R E P I T C
d) N P E

e) E R R U B B
f) H A I R C
g) E R T E A H C
h) O O R D

**3** Now circle the first letter of the word in each word circle.
What are the words?

Example:

**4** Invent your own word circles.

**MIND TWISTERS, PUZZLES & GAMES** — nouns, adjectives

# 2 Countries

**1** What are the countries?

| Picture | **1** Country | **2** Language / Nationality |
|---|---|---|
| a) | France | French |
| b) | | |
| c) | | |
| d) | | |
| e) | | |
| f) | | |

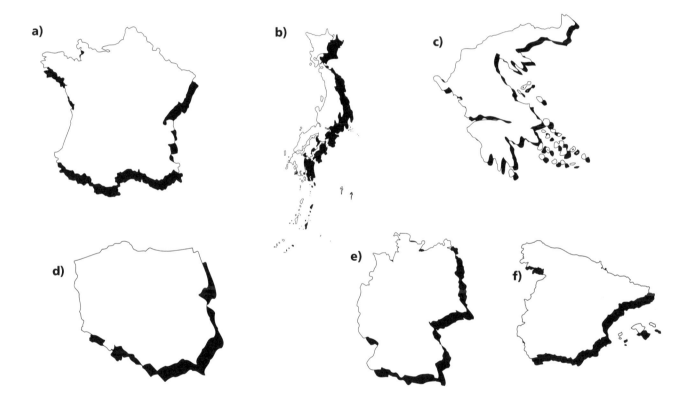

**2** Now write the languages / nationalities.

**3** Work in pairs. Draw three countries.

Show them to each other and guess what they are.

**4** Write two or more countries that:

a) you want to visit ................................. .................................

b) you think are very very beautiful ................................. .................................

c) you think are dangerous ................................. .................................

d) have English as their first language ................................. .................................

e) have very large populations ................................. .................................

MIND TWISTERS, PUZZLES & GAMES  *to be*

# 3 The time

**1) Where are you usually at these times?**

05.00 ..................................................................................................................................

08.00 ..................................................................................................................................

13.00 ..................................................................................................................................

16.00 ..................................................................................................................................

22.00 ..................................................................................................................................

**2) These clocks are reflected in a mirror.**

Underline what time it really is.

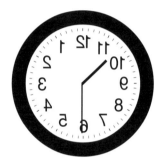

**a)** <u>ten thirty</u> / eleven thirty

**b)** a quarter to nine /
a quarter past nine

**c)** five to nine / five past nine

**d)** twelve o'clock / six o'clock

**e)** ten to four / ten past five

**f)** twenty five past four /
twenty five past five

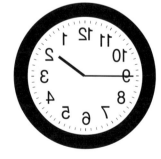

**g)** a quarter to three /
a quarter to two

**3) Work in groups. Solve the brainteaser.**

It takes a grandfather clock 30 seconds to strike 6 o'clock.
How long will it take to strike 12 o'clock?
(The answer is NOT 60 seconds!)

**MIND TWISTERS, PUZZLES & GAMES** ordinal numbers

# 4 Colours

**1)** **Work in pairs.**

What is your favourite colour? ............................................

And your least favourite colour? ............................................

What are good and bad colours for the following:

|  | good | bad |
|---|---|---|
| **a)** your bedroom walls | yellow | purple |
| **b)** a bicycle | | |
| **c)** a T-shirt | | |
| **d)** a car | | |
| **e)** your classroom walls | | |
| **f)** a mobile phone | | |

**2)** **Colour the grid using these colours:**

first row: first box red, second box green, third box brown

second row: first box yellow, second box blue, third box black

third row: first box purple, second box orange, third box pink

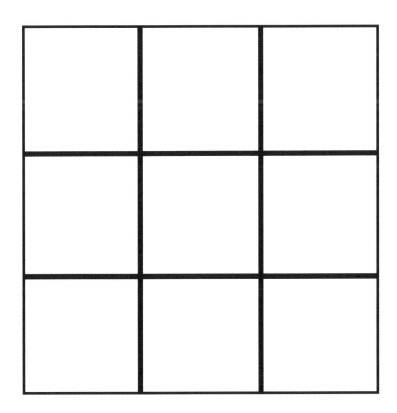

**3)** Place six Xs on the grid without making three in a row in any direction.

**MIND TWISTERS, PUZZLES & GAMES** dates

# 5 The calendar

**1** Write down the months.

a) The month that only has 28 days. ...February...

b) The month that only has 3 letters. ............

c) Three months that begin with 'J'. ............ ............ ............

d) The eighth month of the year. ............

e) The month that begins with an 'S'. ............

f) Two months that have five letters. ............ ............

g) The last month of the year. ............

h) The two months that contain the letter 'o'. ............ ............

## In which month is:

your birthday? ............

your best friend's birthday? ............

your mother's birthday? ............

**2** Solve the brainteaser!

There are 50 students in one classroom.
What is the probability that two people have the same birthday:

a) 3 in 100   b) 97 in 100?

And in a class of just 25 students:

a) 1 in 100   b) 50 in 100?

**MIND TWISTERS, PUZZLES & GAMES**  there is, there are, how many?

# 6 Spot the difference A

**Work in pairs. Your partner has a very similar picture to your picture. But there are 10 differences. Ask questions to find the differences.**

Example:
> Is there a television in your room?
> Yes, there is.
> Is it on or off?

**MIND TWISTERS, PUZZLES & GAMES** — there is, there are, how many?

# 6 Spot the difference B

**Work in pairs. Your partner has a very similar picture to your picture. But there are 10 differences. Ask questions to find the differences.**

Example:
> *Is there a television in your room?*
> *Yes, there is.*
> *Is it on or off?*

MIND TWISTERS, PUZZLES & GAMES   present simple, can

# 7 Habits

**1** Match the words below with the pictures.

a) computer

b) football

c) glasses

d) ice cream

e) mobile phone

f) newspaper

g) piano

h) skis

i) television

j) tennis racket

1 [i]  2 [ ]  3 [ ]  4 [ ]  5 [ ]  6 [ ]  7 [ ]  8 [ ]  9 [ ]  10 [ ]

**2** Now use the words to write ten questions in the present simple.

Write each question on a different piece of paper.

Examples:  *Do you play the piano?*   *Can you ski?*

**3** Your teacher will now tell you how to play the Question Game.

MIND TWISTERS, PUZZLES & GAMES   possessives

# 8 The human face

**1** Match the parts of the body (1-5) with the definitions (a-e).

1 mouth    a) what you see with

2 eyes    b) what you hear with

3 nose    c) what you eat with

4 hair    d) what you smell with

5 ears    e) what is on top of your head

1 [c]  2 [ ]  3 [ ]  4 [ ]  5 [ ]

**2** Work in groups. Look at the picture.

What can you see – a young woman or an old woman?

**3** Work in pairs.

Write the parts of the face: single lines for the young woman, double lines for the old woman.

**4** Read.

What does it mean?
- If you see a young woman, you are: trendy, friendly, extrovert.
- If you see an old woman, you are: traditional, wise, interesting, introvert.
- If you see both the young and the old woman, you are: a genius!

What are *you*?

**MIND TWISTERS, PUZZLES & GAMES**  there is, there are

# 9 Rooms

**1** Match the rooms rooms (1-7) with with their uses (a-g).

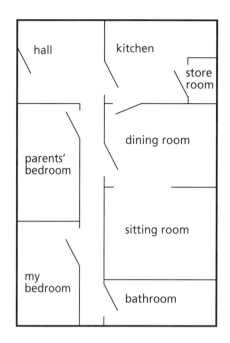

1 bedroom    a) where you wash
2 bathroom    b) where you eat
3 sitting room    c) where you sleep
4 kitchen    d) where you keep things
5 dining room    e) where you go into your house
6 hall    f) where you relax
7 store room    g) where you cook

1 [c]  2 [ ]  3 [ ]  4 [ ]  5 [ ]  6 [ ]  7 [ ]

**2** Draw a plan of your house / apartment, as in the example.

**3** Now work in groups.

a) Pass your plan to the next student. Then write a description of the plan you are given.
b) Pass your description to the next student. Then draw a plan from the description you are given.
c) Compare your original plan with the final plan of your house / apartment. How different are they?

**4** Find your way.

The apartment below has nine rooms (A to I).
Starting and finishing from the outside, visit each room at least once.
You must not go through the same door twice.

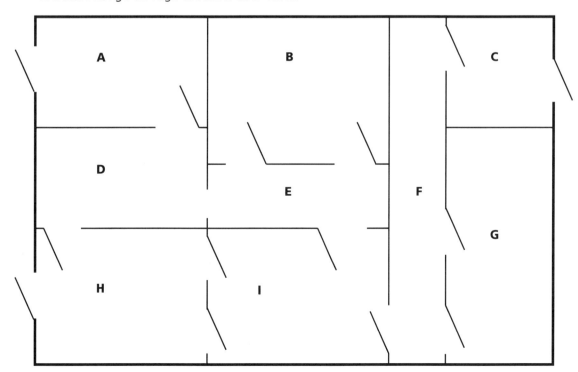

MIND TWISTERS, PUZZLES AND GAMES © MARY GLASGOW MAGAZINES, AN IMPRINT OF SCHOLASTIC INC.

# 10 Picture puzzles

**Work in pairs. Discuss how to solve these puzzles.**

**1)** Look at these glasses.

The 3 glasses on the left are full of orange juice.
The 3 glasses on the right are empty.
Move just one glass so that the glasses are alternately full and empty.

**2)** Look at the 2 arrows.

Using only 2 straight lines, make a third arrow.

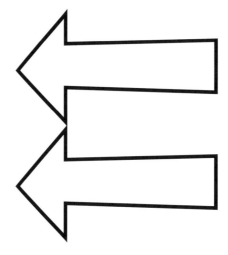

**3)** Use 10 coins to make the triangle.

Now turn the triangle upside-down by moving only 3 coins.

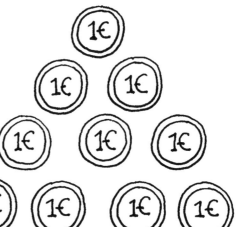

# 11 Smileys

**1** Match the pictures with the people and animals.

a) clown [2]
b) frog [ ]
c) pig [ ]
d) Pinnochio [ ]
e) pipe smoker [ ]
f) punk [ ]
g) Santa Claus, Father Christmas [ ]
h) skateboarder [ ]
i) very unhappy person [ ]
j) wearing glasses [ ]

**2** Work in pairs. Match the smileys with the people and animals.

1. (:-(  [i]
2. *<):o) [ ]
3. *<| :-)> [ ]
4. :---) [ ]
5. :-? [ ]
6. o[-<]: [ ]
7. :8) [ ]
8. 8-) [ ]
9. =:-) [ ]
10. 8) [ ]

MIND TWISTERS, PUZZLES & GAMES   not...enough, too

# 12 Quantities

**1** Write *not* ............... *enough*, *too* ................ , or *correct* in the spaces, as in the examples.

Examples:

How long was the longest human nose on earth?

**a)** 9 centimetres ...*not long enough*...  **b)** 19 cm ............*correct*............  **c)** 29 cm ............*too long*............

How large is the largest human belly?

**a)** 137 centimetres ............*correct*............  **b)** 157 cm ............*too large*............  **c)** 177 cm ............*too large*............

**1** How heavy was the heaviest man on earth?

**a)** 300 kilos ............................  **b)** 400 kg ............................  **c)** 600 kg ............................

**2** How tall was the tallest woman on earth?

**a)** 2.0 metres ............................  **b)** 2.5 m ............................  **c)** 2.8m ............................

**3** How long are the longest human legs on earth?

**a)** 125 centimetres ............................  **b)** 150 cm ............................  **c)** 175 cm ............................

**4** How old was the oldest person on earth?

**a)** 112 years old ............................  **b)** 122 ............................  **c)** 132 ............................

**5** How young is the youngest graduate (someone who has finished university)?

**a)** 10 ............................  **b)** 12 ............................  **c)** 14 ............................

Do the right answers surprise you?

**2** Now look at these pictures and write an appropriate phrase, as in the example.

**1** ...*not enough beds*...   **2** ............................   **3** ............................

**4** ............................   **5** ............................   **6** ............................

# 13 Geography

**1** Underline the correct adjective and then form a comparison.

Example: Russia is (<u>big</u> / small) than the United States. ..... *bigger* ..........

a) The Nile is (long / short) than the Amazon. ...........................

b) The Pacific Ocean is (deep / shallow) than the Atlantic. ...........................

c) K2 is (high / low) than Everest. ...........................

d) Great Britain is a (large / small) island than Greenland. ...........................

e) China has a (long / short) border than Russia. ...........................

f) The population of Africa is (old / young) than the population of Europe. ...........................

g) New York has (short / tall) buildings than Washington. ...........................

h) Tokyo is a (little / much) populated city than Calcutta. ...........................

i) Sydney is (close to / far from) London than Mexico City. ...........................

j) California has a (bad / good) crime rate than Texas. ...........................

**2** Put the words below into the spaces.

Then work in pairs and decide if the statements are are true (**T**) or false (**F**).

> biggest, fewest, greatest, hardest, highest, ~~hottest~~, longest, most, richest, strongest

a) Africa has the ....... *hottest* ....... temperatures in the world. **T** / F

b) Most of the ........................... hurricanes are on the west coast of the USA. T / F

c) The continent with the ........................... states is Europe. T / F

d) English has the ........................... number of speakers throughout the world. T / F

e) Africa is the continent with the ........................... telephones. T / F

f) The country where people generally live the ........................... is Japan. T / F

g) One of the countries with the ........................... calorie consumption is the USA. T / F

h) Turkey is not one of the ........................... producers of turkeys. T / F

i) None of the ........................... countries in the world are in the southern hemisphere. T / F

j) Women work the ........................... in the home in countries in the northern hemisphere. T / F

**MIND TWISTERS, PUZZLES & GAMES** — how much? how many?

# 14 Food and drink  A

**Look at your picture for one minute. Try to remember as much as you can.**

Your partner will now give you his / her picture. Ask questions to test your partner's memory. Then give your picture to your partner.

Examples:

Question: *How **much** brea**d** is there?* Answer: *There is one kilo of bread.*

Question: *How **many** bottle**s** of water are there?* Answer: *There are four bottles of water.*

MIND TWISTERS, PUZZLES & GAMES   how much? how many?

# 14 Food and drink  B

**Look at your picture for one minute. Try to remember as much as you can.**

Now give your picture to your partner. Your partner will ask you questions to test your memory. Now it's your turn! Take your partner's picture and ask questions to test your partner's memory.

Examples:

Question: *How **much** brea**d** is there?* Answer: *There is one kilo of bread.*

Question: *How **many** bottle**s** of water are there?* Answer: *There are four bottles of water.*

# 15 Crazy conundrums

**1** Match the prepositions to the diagrams.

a) next to  [2]
b) towards  [ ]
c) under  [ ]
d) in front of  [ ]
e) at  [ ]
f) behind  [ ]

**2** Put prepositions into the correct spaces.

a) There are three mice in a box all facing the same direction.

The first mouse says: 'There are two mice **(1)** ......behind...... me.'

The second mouse says: 'There is one mouse **(2)** ..................... me and one mouse **(3)** ..................... me.'

The third mouse says: 'There are two mice **(4)** ..................... me and two mice **(5)** ..................... me.'

There are no mirrors in the box.

Explain.

b) There are three large people standing **(6)** ..................... each other **(7)** ..................... one small umbrella. But no one gets wet.

How is this possible?

c) There is a man is dressed entirely in black, wearing a black mask and standing **(8)** ..................... a bus stop. There is a blackout and none of the street lights are on. Suddenly the man decides to cross the road. At the same time a car, with no headlights on, comes very fast **(9)** ..................... the man. But the car easily turns in time and doesn't hit the man. How does the driver manage not to hit the man?

**3** Work in groups. Solve the three conundrums.

MIND TWISTERS, PUZZLES & GAMES   male *vs* female

# 16 Family members

**1** Complete the family tree with these words:

daughter
father
grandmother
grandfather
son

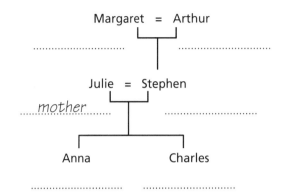

**2** Put these words into the correct place in the circles.

~~aunt~~, baby, ~~brother~~, children, ~~cousin~~, daughter, nephew, niece, sister, son, uncle

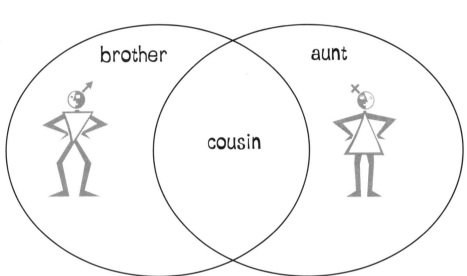

**3** Work in groups. How many of these brainteasers can you solve?

a) Three women walk into a room: two mothers and two daughters. Explain.

b) A brother is three times as old as his sister. But in four years, he will only be twice as old. How old is the brother now?

c) **Girl**: Are you sure Mr Jones is your uncle?
**Boy**: Yes, and I am his uncle!
**Girl**: So you are his nephew and he is your nephew!
**Boy**: That's right.
Explain.

d) Emma met Cristina in the street. 'I'm sure I know you.' 'You certainly do know me,' replied Cristina. 'Your mother was my mother's only daughter.' How are they related?

e) A brother and sister are in the supermarket. The brother points at a boy and says: 'That boy is my nephew.' But his sister says: 'Well, he isn't my nephew.' Explain.

f) If a group of people contains: a father, a mother, an uncle, an aunt, a sister, a brother, a nephew, a niece and two cousins, what is the smallest number of people they can be?

**Score: how many did you get right?**

1 not very good
2 satisfactory
3 good
4 excellent
5 genius
6 you've seen the answers!

# 17 Jail break

**Put the words in the box into the spaces. Then resolve the problem.**

> can, can, cannot, cannot, must, must

The prison has 36 cells in it. You are a prisoner in cell X and you want to escape. You also want to release all the other prisoners. So before you **(1)** ...can... escape you **(2)** ............... visit every cell once. You **(3)** ............... go back into any cell that you have already visited, apart from cell X. You **(4)** ............... go out of a cell from any of its four walls, but you **(5)** ............... go out from its corners. And, of course, the final way out **(6)** ............... be through cell Y.

# 18 Coin game

**Follow the instructions.**

Take eight coins – four big ones and four small ones.

Place the coins as in the first picture.

Your aim is to finish with the coins as in the second picture by moving two coins at a time.

You *must* move two coins at a time, you cannot just move one.
The coins you move *must* be next to each other.

When moving, you can jump over as many other coins as you want; but you must always move two coins together and keep them in the same order.

So, if you move a big coin and a small coin together, and the big coin is on the left and the small coin is on the right, you must put them down with the big coin still on the left and the small coin still on the right.

## You can solve the problem in only four moves.

**MIND TWISTERS, PUZZLES & GAMES** opinions

# 19 Work it out

**1** Work in pairs or groups. Look at these pictures. What are they?

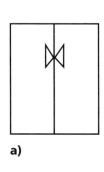
a)

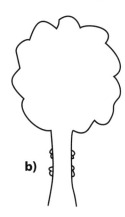
b)

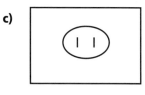
c)

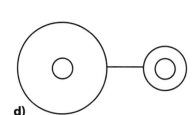
d)

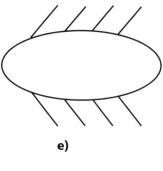
e)

a) ......................................................................................................................................
b) ......................................................................................................................................
c) ......................................................................................................................................
d) ......................................................................................................................................
e) ......................................................................................................................................

**2** Work in pairs or groups. Look at these four pictures and answer the questions about them.

a) A cock has laid this egg. Which side of the mountain will it fall?

b) Between the boy and the cherry tree is a river with very thin ice on it. How does the boy get the cherries?

c) Which bull will give more milk?

d) Which is the biggest cross?

a)

b)

c)

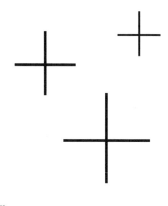
d)

MIND TWISTERS, PUZZLES & GAMES   must

# 20 Numbers

**1) Solve the problem.**

To get into a top-security prison you must say the password to the guard.
There is a certain system that you must follow:

If the guard says 1, 2, 6 or 10, you must say 'three'.
If he says 4, 5 or 9, you must say 'four'.
If he says 3, 7 or 8, you must say 'five'.
If he says 11 or 12, you must say 'six'.
What must you say if he says 13?

**2) Complete the grid.**

To complete this grid, put one of the other numbers from 1 to 9 in each space. Use each number once.

The total of each line, horizontal ( ––– ), vertical ( | ) or diagonal ( / \ ), must add up to 15.

**MIND TWISTERS, PUZZLES & GAMES** — some, any

# 21 School bus

**1) Read.**

Every day a girl takes the bus to school. She can get off the bus at two stops. The first one is 100 metres before her school. The second stop is 200 metres after her school. She always rides past the first stop and gets off at the second.

**2) Read these explanations and underline *some* or *any* in each sentence.**

|  | very | quite | not at all |
|---|---|---|---|
| a) She doesn't want to get to school on time, because she still has <u>some</u> / any homework to do. | ☐ | ☐ | ☐ |
| b) Her boyfriend comes from the opposite direction. He gets off at the same stop as her and always needs to give her *something* / *anything*. | ☐ | ☐ | ☐ |
| c) Her school is a school just for girls; it doesn't have *some* / *any* boys. | ☐ | ☐ | ☐ |
| d) She doesn't have *some* / *any* lessons in the first hour. | ☐ | ☐ | ☐ |
| e) It doesn't cost her *some* / *any* more money to get off at the second stop. | ☐ | ☐ | ☐ |
| f) Her school is half way up a hill and she doesn't want to do *some* / *any* exercise. | ☐ | ☐ | ☐ |
| g) It's Sunday and there isn't *someone* / *anyone* there. | ☐ | ☐ | ☐ |
| h) She doesn't want to arrive at school early because there are *some* / *any* people that she doesn't like who wait for her outside the entrance. | ☐ | ☐ | ☐ |
| i) She doesn't have *some* / *any* friends. | ☐ | ☐ | ☐ |

**3) Work in groups.**

Put ticks in the boxes to show how relevant the explanations are:

- very relevant
- quite relevant
- not at all relevant

Your teacher will then give you the 'correct' solution.

**MIND TWISTERS, PUZZLES & GAMES** *it vs one*

# 22 Guess the object

**1)** Work in pairs or groups. Look at the photos. What are the objects?

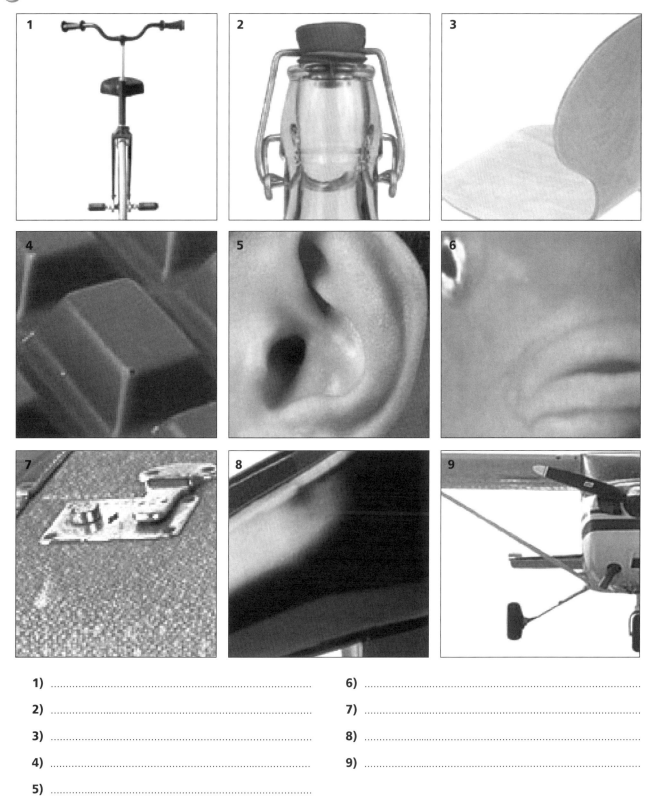

1) ..................................................
2) ..................................................
3) ..................................................
4) ..................................................
5) ..................................................
6) ..................................................
7) ..................................................
8) ..................................................
9) ..................................................

**2)** Work in groups. Play this game.

One person thinks of an object. The others ask a total of 20 *yes* / *no* questions to discover what the object is. Think carefully about your questions – the answers can only be 'yes' or 'no' – nothing else.

**MIND TWISTERS, PUZZLES & GAMES** — superlatives, present perfect

# 23 Experiences

**1** Put the adjectives in italics into the superlative form.

Examples:

What's the ........*longest*...... you've ever had your hair? *long*

What's the ...*most wonderful*... holiday you've ever had? *wonderful*

a) What's the ........................... mistake you've ever made? *big*

b) What's the ........................... video game you've ever played? *good*

c) What's the ........................... day you've ever had? *happy*

d) What's the ........................... you've ever been away from home? *far*

e) What's the ........................... experience you've ever had? *terrifying*

f) What's the ........................... point you've ever been to? *high*

g) What's the ........................... speed you've ever travelled at? *fast*

h) What's the ........................... thing you've ever bought? *expensive*

i) What's the ........................... meal you've ever had? *delicious*

j) What's the ........................... movie you've ever seen? *bad*

**2** Write answers to three of the questions in **1**.

...........................................................................................................................................................

...........................................................................................................................................................

...........................................................................................................................................................

**3** Work in pairs.

Read and memorize the questions in **1**.
Now take it in turns. One of you reads out an answer. The other one must say the question that matches the answers.

Example:

Your partner: *Australia.*

You: *What's the furthest you've ever been away from home?*

**4** Work in pairs.

Write two questions using the superlative of some of the following adjectives.
Then ask your partner your questions.

( beautiful   boring   exciting   fat   incredible   interesting   ridiculous   silly   strong )

...........................................................................................................................................?

...........................................................................................................................................?

MIND TWISTERS, PUZZLES & GAMES   will

# 24 High numbers A

**1** What do you think?

In your lifetime:

1  How many times will your heart beat?

   **a)** 2 million     **b)** 20 million     **c)** 200 million     **d)** 2,000 million

2  How many years will you spend on the Internet?

   **a)** 2 months     **b)** 2 years     **c)** 12 years     **d)** 22 years

3  How many times will you eat at a fast food restaurant?

   **a)** 18 times     **b)** 81     **c)** 1,811     **d)** 18,111

4  How many times will you hear the words 'I love you'?

   **a)** 34 times     **b)** 348     **c)** 3,480     **d)** 30,348

**2** Guess the missing information.

The numbers below refer to how many times we will do certain things in our lifetime. Try to guess the missing information and then ask your partner for the correct number. You begin the exercise.

Example:

*You*: *I think I will blink a trillion times, but how many times will I blink?*

*Your partner*: *You will blink 00000 times. I think I will eat 00000 loaves of bread, but …. etc.*

I will blink .................. times.

You will eat 7,800 loaves of bread.

I will flush the toilet .................. times.

You will lose 136 kilogrammes of skin.

I will spend .................. years sleeping.

You will take 13,650 baths or showers.

I will use .................. toilet rolls.

You will walk 240,000 kilometres.

I will watch .................. years of TV.

You will wear 675 pairs of underpants.

**MIND TWISTERS, PUZZLES & GAMES**  *will*

# 24 High numbers B

**1** What do you think?

In your lifetime:

1 How many times will your heart beat?
   a) 2 million      b) 20 million      c) 200 million      d) 2,000 million

2 How many years will you spend on the Internet?
   a) 2 months      b) 2 years      c) 12 years      d) 22 years

3 How many times will you eat at a fast food restaurant?
   a) 18 times      b) 81      c) 1,811      d) 18,111

4 How many times will you hear the words 'I love you'?
   a) 34 times      b) 348      c) 3,480      d) 30,348

**2** Guess the missing information.

The numbers below refer to how many times we will do certain things in our lifetime. Try to guess the missing information and then ask your partner for the correct number. Your partner will begin the exercise.

Example:

*Your partner*: I think I will blink a trillion times, but how many times will I blink?

*You*: You will blink 682 million times. I think I will eat 500 loaves of bread, but how many will I eat?

*Your partner*: You will eat 00000 loaves of bread. I think I will flush the toilet 00000 times but ... etc.

You will blink 682 million times.

I will eat ............... loaves of bread.

You will flush the toilet 109,200 times.

I will lose ............... kilogrammes of skin.

You will spend 25 years sleeping.

I will take ............... baths or showers.

You will use 2,574 toilet rolls.

I will walk ............... kilometres.

You will watch 12 years of TV.

I will wear ............... pairs of underpants.

**MIND TWISTERS, PUZZLES & GAMES** — imperative

# 25 Number games A

**1) Put these verbs into the spaces:**

> add, add, divide, don't tell, double, subtract, think

a) ...Think... of a number, and remember it!   Example: 5

b) .................. me what it is.

c) .................. 1.   5 - 1 = 4

d) .................. the result.   4 x 2 = 8

e) .................. the first number you thought of.   8 + 5 = 13

f) Now .................. 2.   13 + 2 = 15

g) Then .................. by 3.   15 / 3 = 5

The result is the number you first thought of.

**2) Now work in pairs.**

Try the game on your partner, and your partner will do a game on you.

**3) Work in pairs.**

Now do this game on your partner, and your partner will do another game on you.

Think of a number, and remember it!   Example: 6

Add its successor (the number after it).   6 + 7 = 13

Add nine.   13 + 9 = 22

Divide by two.   22 / 2 = 11

Subtract your original number.   11 − 6 = 5

The result is 5. (The result is always 5.)

# 25 Number games B

**1) Put these verbs into the spaces:**

> add, divide, don't tell, multiply, subtract, subtract, ~~think~~

a) ......Think...... of a number, and remember it!    Example: 5

b) .................... me what it is.

c) .................... 3.                              5 + 3 = 8

d) .................... by 2.                          8 × 2 = 16

e) .................... 4.                             16 - 4 = 12

f) .................... by 2.                          12 / 2 = 6

g) Now .................... the number you first thought of.  6 − 5 = 1

The result is 1. (The result is always 1.)

**2) Now work in pairs.**

Try the game on your partner, and your partner will do a game on you.

**3) Work in pairs.**

Now do this game on your partner, and your partner will do another game on you.

Think of a number, and remember it!    Example: 10

Add 7.                                  10 + 7 = 17

Multiply by 2.                          17 × 2 = 34

Add 12.                                 34 + 12 = 46

Divide by 2.                            46 / 2 = 23

Subtract the original number.           23 − 10 = 13

The result is 13. (The result is always 13.)

**MIND TWISTERS, PUZZLES & GAMES** first conditional

# 26 Farmer's dilemma

**1) Read.**

A farmer has a dog, a sheep and a bale of hay.

The farmer needs to cross a river. But his boat is very small.

He can only take one animal or the hay with him.

If he leaves the dog alone with the sheep, the dog will attack the sheep.

If he leaves the sheep alone with the hay, the sheep will eat the hay.

**2) Work in groups.**

How does the farmer resolve the problem?

**3) Finish these sentences.**

a) If I don't do my homework tonight, ...my teacher will be cross with me......................... .

b) If I talk during today's lesson, ......................................................................... .

c) If my mobile phone rings now, ......................................................................... .

d) I will go to the cinema tonight if ......................................................................... .

e) I will go to university if ......................................................................... .

f) My parents will get very angry if ......................................................................... .

**4) Work in pairs.**

Read out just the endings of your sentences in 3.
Your partner has to guess the beginning.

**MIND TWISTERS, PUZZLES & GAMES** *can, can't*

# 27 School jokes

**Match the jokes with the cartoons. Then put *can* or *can't* into the spaces.**

a) *Teacher*: Really! I know children who are three years old who ……*can*…… solve this problem.
*Pupil*: Well, that's the trouble – I'm thirteen.

b) *Pupil*: How …………………… I improve my guitar playing?
*Teacher*: Leave it in its case.

c) *Teacher*: Caterina, you know you …………………… sleep in my class.
*Caterina*: You're right, but maybe if you were a little quieter I could.

d) *Pupil*: What's the difference between a boring teacher and a boring book?
*Another pupil*: You …………………… shut the book up.

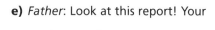

e) *Father*: Look at this report! Your teacher says he …………………… teach you anything!
*Pupil*: I told you he is a terrible teacher.

f) *Teacher*: …………………… anybody tell me which days begin with the letter 'T'?
*Pupil*: Today and tomorrow.

**MIND TWISTERS, PUZZLES & GAMES** — present simple, present continuous

# 28 Teacher jokes

**1** Read these jokes and underline the correct form of the verb.

a) *Teacher*: What <u>comes</u> / *is coming* before eight?
*Pupil*: My school bus, usually.

b) *Teacher*: *Do you chew* / *Are you chewing* gum?
*Pupil*: No, I'm Henry Taylor.

c) *Teacher*: Charles, *do you copy* / *are you copying* Martin's answers?
*Pupil*: No, Miss, I *just check* / *am just checking* to see if his answers are correct.

d) *Pupil*: What *do you call* / *are you calling* someone who keeps talking when people have stopped listening?
*Another pupil*: A teacher.

e) *Pupil*: What's the difference between teachers and chocolate?
*Another pupil*: Children *like* / *are liking* chocolate.

f) *Teacher*: Harry, how *do you manage* / *are you managing* to get so many things wrong in a day?
*Pupil*: Because I *arrive* / *am arriving* here early, Miss.

**2** Work in pairs.

Each line below is one line from a joke or riddle.
Put the lines together to make two other complete jokes.

Example:

a) *Why is it that you always find something in the last place you look?*

f) *Because when you find it, you stop looking.*

~~a)~~ Why is it that you always find something in the last place you look?

b) What is everyone in the world doing at this very moment?

c) What are you writing, Simon?

d) I don't know, I won't receive it until tomorrow.

e) Growing older.

~~f)~~ Because when you find it, you stop looking.

g) And what does it say?

h) A letter to myself, Miss.

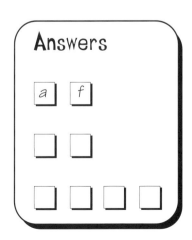

# 29 Lift mystery

**1) Read this story.**

Joe lives on the 20th floor of a block of flats in London. Every day when he leaves his flat to go to work at the bank, he gets in the lift on the 20th floor and gets out on the ground floor.

When he returns home from the bank, he gets in the lift on the ground floor, but he gets out at the 13th floor and walks up the stairs to the 20th floor.

## Why?

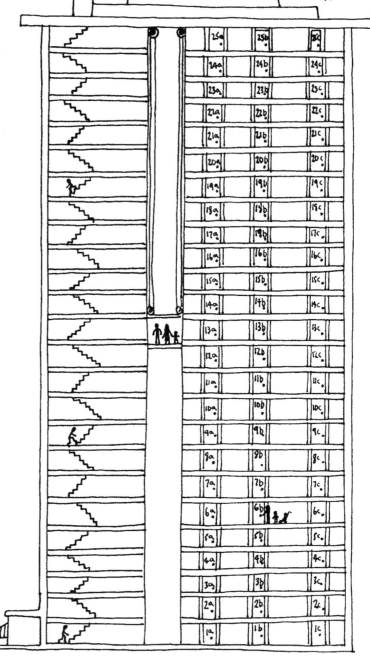

**2) Try to memorize these questions.**

Does he know someone on the 13th floor?

Does he want to do some exercise?

Is he superstitious?

Does he suffer from vertigo or claustrophobia?

Does the lift go from the 13th floor to the 20th floor?

Is it relevant that he works in a bank?

Does he always get out of the lift at the 13th floor?

If he's not alone in the lift, does he get out at the 13th floor?

Does he have a particular problem?

**3) Work in groups.**

Ask questions to find the answer to the problem.

**MIND TWISTERS, PUZZLES & GAMES** present continuous

# 30 Chatline acronyms

**1** Chat about chatlines.

Do you use chatlines?
How often? Who do you chat with?

**2** Match the phrases with the cartoons.

a) I am rolling on the floor laughing

1 [ h ]

b) My parents are listening

2 [ ]

c) I am thinking of you

3 [ ]

4 [ ]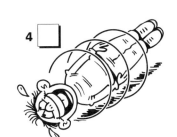

d) I am hanging my head in shame

e) Ha ha I'm only only joking

5 [ ]

f) I am laughing my head off

7 [ ]

6 [ ]

g) I am smiling ear to ear

8 [ ]

h) I am crying real big tears

**3** Match the acronyms below with the phrases in 2.

1 hhis    2 crbt    3 hhoj    4 lho
5 pal    6 rotfl    7 sete    8 toy

1 [ d ]  2 [ ]  3 [ ]  4 [ ]  5 [ ]  6 [ ]  7 [ ]  8 [ ]

# 31 Riddles

**1** Can you solve this ancient riddle?

As long as I eat, I live – but when I drink, I die. What am I?

**2** Put the verbs from the box into the spaces.

> becomes   comes   ~~goes~~   has   has   holds   is   moves   spell   use

a) What ......*goes*...... round the house and in the house but never touches the house?

b) What is yours but others .............................. more than you?

c) What .............................. once in a minute, twice in a moment, but never in a thousand years?

d) What is it that is lighter than what it .............................. made of and more of it is hidden than is seen?

e) What do you use in the bathroom that .............................. water but is full of holes?

f) What .............................. 50 heads but can't think?

g) What .............................. bigger the more you take away from it?

h) What word does every dictionary .............................. incorrectly?

i) What turns everything round but never .............................. ?

j) What .............................. 50 legs but can't walk?

**3** Work in groups.

Can you work out the answers to **2**?
If you can't, then match each question to one of the pictures below.

| a | 1 | b | | c | | d | | e | | f | | g | | h | | i | | j | |

**MIND TWISTERS, PUZZLES & GAMES** imperative

# 32 Giving directions

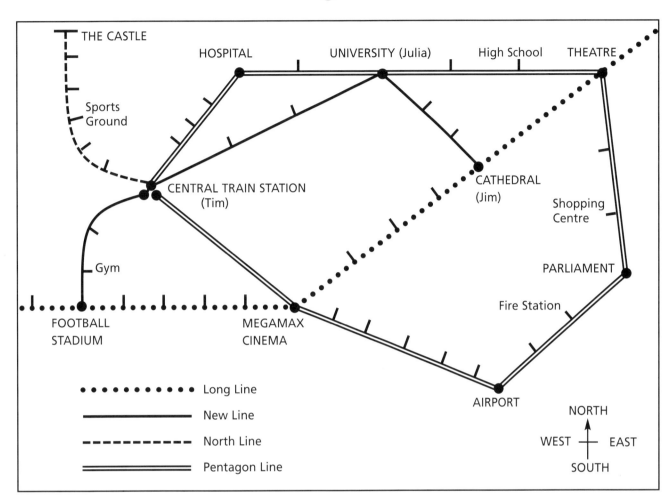

**1) Read and answer the question.**

Julia lives near the university. She has two boyfriends: Tim and Jim. Tim lives near the Central Train Station, Jim lives near the Cathedral. When she goes to see them, she travels on the underground. She loves them both equally. So Julia invents a way to see either Tim or Jim without deciding before which one she is going to see. In this way she will show no preference for one of them in particular. The trains for the Central Train Station and for the Cathedral leave from the same platform. Both trains leave at intervals of ten minutes. Julia doesn't have a watch or a mobile phone so she doesn't know what time it is when she arrives at the platform, and there are no clocks at the station. She then takes the first train that arrives – she doesn't know if this train will be for the Central Train Station or the Cathedral. But 90% of the time she goes to the Central Train Station.

Why?

**2) Work in pairs.**

You are at the Central Train Station. Choose another station on the map. Don't tell your partner. Now direct your partner to the station without saying the names of any stations.

Example:

*Take the Pentagon Line going north. Get off at the sixth stop and get on the New Line going south-east. Get off at the third stop. Where are you?*

Answer: *Cathedral.*

**MIND TWISTERS, PUZZLES & GAMES** — irregular verbs, past simple, present perfect

# 33 Ask the teacher

**1** Write the past simple and past participle of these irregular verbs.

a) be ....was........ ....been........  f) have ................ ................
b) break ................ ................  g) lose ................ ................
c) do ................ ................  h) meet ................ ................
d) drive ................ ................  i) see ................ ................
e) fall ................ ................  j) take ................ ................

**2** Work in pairs.

Now use the verbs and the phrases below to make personal questions to your teacher. Add two questions of your own at the bottom. The questions must begin:

*Have you ever …. ?*
or
*Did you … when you were younger?*
(for something finished in the past)

Examples:

*Have you ever been to America?*
*Were you a girl guide when you were younger?*

a ghost?

| | | | |
|---|---|---|---|
| to America | a | b | c |
| a scout / girl guide | a | b | c |
| a ghost | a | b | c |
| a different job before becoming a teacher | a | b | c |
| to university | a | b | c |
| part in a marathon | a | b | c |
| asleep during a lesson | a | b | c |
| much faster than the speed limit | a | b | c |
| someone famous | a | b | c |
| something expensive | a | b | c |
| your wallet / purse | a | b | c |
| on television | a | b | c |
| long hair | a | b | c |
| ................................ | a | b | c |
| ................................ | a | b | c |

a different job?

long hair?

asleep during a lesson?

**3** Work in pairs.

Before you ask your teacher the questions, think about her / his answers.
Will the answer be: **a)** certainly **b)** perhaps **c)** definitely not? Circle the answers you think.

**4** Now ask your teacher the questions and check your answers to 3.

Are you surprised???!

# 34 Visual game

**1) Work in pairs.**

First read all three puzzles (**a**, **b**, **c**) below and decide how many minutes you think it will take to solve them. You have a maximum of five minutes for each one. For each puzzle, put a mark in one of these boxes 1–5.

a)  1 ☐  2 ☐  3 ☐  4 ☐  5 ☐

b)  1 ☐  2 ☐  3 ☐  4 ☐  5 ☐

c)  1 ☐  2 ☐  3 ☐  4 ☐  5 ☐

**a)** These four matches represent the shape of a wheelbarrow with a plant inside. Leaving the plant where it is, move two matches to remake the wheelbarrow so that the plant is outside the wheelbarrow.

Use four matches (or pens) and a coin to make the wheelbarrow and plant.

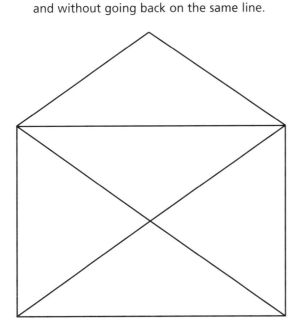

**b)** Draw this envelope with one continuous line and without going back on the same line.

**c)** Use twelve matches (or pens) to make the picture below.

Now move three matches to new positions to make three squares.

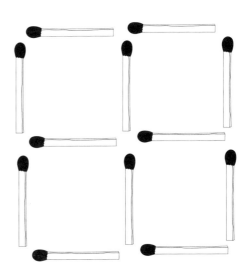

**2) Work in pairs. Now do the games and see how long it really takes!**

**MIND TWISTERS, PUZZLES & GAMES** — irregular verbs

# 35 Horse race

**1** Look at these irregular verbs.

Correct the ones which contain a mistake.

Example:

|  | take | ~~toke~~ | taken | ......*took*...... |
|---|---|---|---|---|
| a) | become | become | became | .................. |
| b) | chose | chose | chosen | .................. |
| c) | cost | costed | costed | .................. |
| d) | fall | felt | felt | .................. |
| e) | find | founded | founded | .................. |
| f) | give | gave | given | .................. |
| g) | know | knew | known | .................. |
| h) | meet | met | met | .................. |
| i) | ride | rode | ridden | .................. |
| j) | teach | teached | teached | .................. |

**2** Put these verbs into the text in the simple past.

> 1 make  2 ride  3 begin  4 get  5 come  6 say  7 get  8 win

Two friends decided to have a horse race. They (**1**) ..........*made*........ up new rules: the horse which crosses the line first loses the race. So they started the race and (**2**) .................. very slowly towards the finishing line. They stopped about 20 metres from the finishing line. They (**3**) .................. to wonder how they could finish the race and they (**4**) .................. off their horses. Then a girl friend (**5**) .................. to talk them. She (**6**) .................. something to both of them and immediately they both (**7**) .................. on a horse. Then they galloped very fast towards the finishing line and one of them (**8**) .................. the race.

**3** Work in groups.

What did the girl friend say to the two men?

**MIND TWISTERS, PUZZLES & GAMES**  first conditional and temporal clauses

# 36 Maths

**1)** Underline the correct form of the verbs in italics.

**a)** If a cat and a half *eat* / *will eat* a mouse and a half in an hour and a half, how long will it take ten cats to eat ten mice?

**b)** If an old electric train *is going* / *will go* east at 80 km an hour and the wind *is blowing* / *will blow* from the south at 40 km an hour, which way will the smoke from the train blow?

**c)** You have a ten-volume set of encyclopaedias, which are arranged in numerical order on your desk. The cover of each volume is 3mm thick and the pages take up 3cm. If a bookworm *starts* / *will start* on page 1 of Volume 1 and *stops* / *will stop* on the last page of Volume 2, how many centimetres will it travel?

**d)** You are getting ready to go to the disco. You are just about to take some socks out of your drawer when the electricity goes off and you can't see anything. In your drawer there are only red and blue socks. How many socks *do* / *will* you have to take out before you *get* / *will get* two socks of the same colour?

**e)** Farmer Giles has six and a half haystacks on one side of his field and seven and a half haystacks on the other side of his field. If he *puts* / *will put* them together, how many haystacks *does* / *will* he have?

**f)** A train that is 1 km long is moving at 60 km an hour. It goes into a tunnel that is 1 km long. How long *does* / *will* it take until the train *is* / *will be* out of the tunnel completely?

**2)** Work in pairs or groups.
Answer the questions in **1**.

Score: how many did you get right?
**1-2**: not bad
**3**: quite good
**4**: good
**5**: excellent
**6**: Einstein!

# 37 Silly maths

**Work in pairs to solve the problems.**

Be careful, only one requires a real calculation!

**a)** A horse is tied to a rope which is fifteen metres long.
Twenty metres from the horse is some hay, but the horse is still able to eat it. How?

**b)** If your friend is carrying three sacks of corn on her back and you are carrying four sacks, who is carrying the most weight?

**c)** How many animals did Moses take on his ark?

**d)** An assistant in a butcher's shop is one metre ninety tall.
What does he weigh?

**e)** How much dirt is there in a hole in the ground which measures 1.5m by 3m and is 1m deep?

**f)** Josh's mother has three children: one is called April and one is called May.
What is the other one called?

**g)** Krystal has five letters and five addressed envelopes.
If she puts the letters in the envelopes at random (i.e. without looking at what she is doing), what are the chances that only four letters are in their correct envelopes?

**h)** Seven people arrive at a business meeting.
Each person shakes hands once with each of the others.
How many handshakes does that make?

**MIND TWISTERS, PUZZLES & GAMES** present simple

# 38 Text messaging

 **Work in pairs.**

## Quiz: Are you a mobile maniac?

Do you have a mobile phone?

If you don't have a mobile phone, imagine you are one of your friends who has one.

1. How many mobiles do you have?
   a) one   b) two   c) three   d) four or more

2. When did you buy your first mobile?
   a) last month   b) last year   c) three years ago
   d) more than five years ago

3. What colour is it?
   a) grey or black   b) blue or green   c) red   d) orange or yellow

4. How often do you use it?
   a) once a week   b) once a day   c) four or five times a day
   d) more than once an hour

5. How much do you spend a month on phone calls / messages?
   a) nothing   b) less than most of your friends
   c) the same as your friends   d) more than your friends

6. What percentage of the features / characteristics of your mobile do you know how to use?
   a) 1-25%   b) 50%   c) 75%   d) 100%

7. How many text messages do you send every day?
   a) 1   b) 2-5   c) 6-10   d) 10 +

1 ☐  2 ☐  3 ☐  4 ☐  5 ☐  6 ☐  7 ☐

### Score

**Mostly As:**
you are a technophobe!

**Mostly Bs:**
your parents are probably pleased with the way you use your mobile, but your friends would probably like you to use it more.

**Mostly Cs:**
you're a cool guy!

**Mostly Ds:**
you are a mobile maniac with more money than good sense!

---

**2** Match the text messages with their meanings.

a) bcnu       1 I like you
b) ilq        2 are you alright?
c) oic        3 oh I see
d) ruok       4 be seeing you

a ☐   b ☐   c ☐   d ☐

**3** Work in groups.

Can you work out these text messages?

a) how r u

b) c u l8er 2day

c) r u free 2nite

d) w8 4 me @ the cinema

**MIND TWISTERS, PUZZLES & GAMES** active / passive

# 39 Loch Ness Monster

**1** Read the story below and underline the correct form of the verbs.

The Loch Ness monster exists and last year a super rich Texan *decided* / *was decided* (**1**) to prove it. All his photographic equipment *sent* / *was sent* (**2**) from Texas to Loch Ness, where the Texan and his team *put* / *was put* (**3**) it on an enormous boat. The Texan *spent* / *was spent* (**4**) a week on the Loch waiting for the monster to appear. Suddenly one night there was a terrible crash and the Texan *found* / *was found* (**5**) himself face to face with the monster under the water (unfortunately he didn't have his camera with him). His boat *smashed* / *was smashed* (**6**) to pieces by the monster, and the oil, which powered the boat, leaked onto the Loch. Every day the oil slick *doubled* / *was doubled* (**7**) in size and Scottish environmental groups *became* / *were become* (**8**) very worried. After 64 days half the Loch *covered* / *was covered* (**9**) by the oil slick.

**2** Work in groups.

Read the story again and decide how many more days it took before all the Loch was covered.

**MIND TWISTERS, PUZZLES & GAMES** past simple, past continuous

# 40 Night watchman

**1** Look at the pictures and then put the sentences into the correct order.

a) His boss, Mr Briggs, had an important business meeting in Paris on Wednesday.

b) It was Monday night. Bernard was a night watchman at a bank. His job was to make sure that no one tried to rob the bank.

c) On Thursday morning, Mr Briggs called Bernard to his office and fired him.

d) On Wednesday Mr Briggs had a high temperature and he couldn't go to the meeting.

e) That night Bernard dreamt the plane his boss was flying in to Paris crashed, killing everyone on the plane.

f) The next morning, Bernard told Mr Briggs about his dream. Mr Briggs said nothing.

g) The plane to Paris on Wednesday crashed, killing everyone.

1 [b]  2 [ ]  3 [ ]  4 [ ]  5 [ ]  6 [ ]  7 [ ]

**2** Work in pairs.

Why did Mr Briggs fire Bernard? Complete the answer below.

Mr Briggs fired Bernard, because on Monday night Bernard was ..............................ing

instead of ..............................ing.

# 41 Beastly brainteasers

**1) Work in pairs.**

First read all the puzzles (**a**, **b**, **c**, **d**) below and decide which two are the easiest and which two are the most difficult.

**a)** The Duchess of Sasso Ritto had six pieces of silver chain, with four links in each piece. She went to a jeweller and asked him to make it into one long chain, open at both ends. The jeweller said: 'The cost will depend on how many times I open and close a ring. The more rings I open and the more rings I close, the more it will cost you. So, if I open the end of each chain and link it to the next, that will be ten operations, because each opening is one operation and each closing is one operation.'
The Duchess replied: 'That would cost too much. Please do it in eight operations.'
Did the jeweller manage to do it in eight operations?

**b)** Look at the four lines below. Draw in five more lines to make ten.

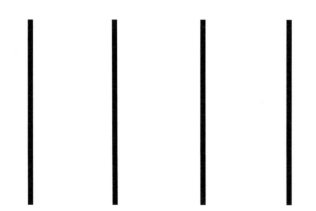

**c)** Use 14 coins and place them along the edges of your desk, so that there are the same number of coins on each edge.

**d)** Make two triangles using five matches or pens.

**2) Work in pairs.**

Now solve the two puzzles which you thought were easiest.

**MIND TWISTERS, PUZZLES & GAMES** past simple, past perfect

# 42 Detectives

**1) Work in groups.**

You are detectives. Look at the picture and decide how Anthony (A) and Cleopatra (C) died.
Note: some details are relevant, others are not relevant.

Imagine your teacher was a witness.
Write down some questions to ask her / him.

**2) As a class, ask your teacher your questions and try to solve the case.**

# 43 Hotel mystery

Look at your picture. Don't show it to anyone else. Describe it to the other students and find out what is in their pictures.
Then decide what order the pictures go in to make a story.

Look at your picture. Don't show it to anyone else. Describe it to the other students and find out what is in their pictures.
Then decide what order the pictures go in to make a story.

Look at your picture. Don't show it to anyone else. Describe it to the other students and find out what is in their pictures.
Then decide what order the pictures go in to make a story.

Look at your picture. Don't show it to anyone else. Describe it to the other students and find out what is in their pictures.
Then decide what order the pictures go in to make a story.

Look at your picture. Don't show it to anyone else. Describe it to the other students and find out what is in their pictures.
Then decide what order the pictures go in to make a story.

**MIND TWISTERS, PUZZLES & GAMES** — imperative

# 44 Doctor jokes

**1)** Match the beginnings of these jokes with their endings.

1  Doctor, doctor! My little girl has swallowed a pen. What can I do?
2  Doctor, doctor! I feel like a yo-yo.
3  Doctor, doctor! I can't stop myself stealing things.
4  Doctor, doctor! Everyone keeps ignoring me.
5  Doctor, doctor! I keep thinking there are two of me.

a) Sit down, sit down, sit down.
b) Don't both talk at once please.
c) Next please.
d) Use a pencil until I get there.
e) Have you taken anything for it?

1 [d]  2 [ ]  3 [ ]  4 [ ]  5 [ ]

**2)** Work in pairs. Decide on the best answer in each joke.

1  Doctor, doctor! I think I'm an apple.
a) Are you red or green?
b) Come over here – I won't bite you.

2  Doctor, doctor! I can't stop talking to myself.
a) I wondered why you were looking so bored.
b) Well shut up then.

3  Doctor, doctor! I get this feeling that no one can hear what I'm saying.
a) What seems to be the trouble?
b) Yes, I know what you mean.

4  Doctor, doctor! I've only got 59 seconds to live.
a) I haven't got all day.
b) Wait a minute please.

5  Doctor, doctor, I keep thinking I'm invisible.
a) Who said that?
b) Well, see an optician.

6  Doctor, doctor. No one believes a word I say.
a) Are you sure?
b) Tell me the truth now, what's your REAL problem?

1 [b]  2 [ ]  3 [ ]
4 [ ]  5 [ ]  6 [ ]

**3)** Work in pairs.

These four 'doctor, doctor' jokes have got muddled up.
Separate them and put them in the correct order. Each one has three lines (first, second, third)

| FIRST LINE | SECOND LINE | THIRD LINE |
|---|---|---|
| a) Doctor, doctor! I keep seeing double. | e) Bring him to see me then. | i) I can't get the top off the bottle. |
| b) Doctor, doctor! I keep seeing fish. | f) Have you seen an optician? | j) I can't, he doesn't stop at your floor. |
| c) Doctor, doctor! My husband thinks he's a lift. | g) Lie on the couch, please. | k) Look I told you, it's fish that I see. |
| d) Doctor, doctor! Those strength pills you gave me aren't doing me any good. | h) Why not? | l) Which one? |

1 [a] [g] [l]   2 [ ] [ ] [ ]   3 [ ] [ ] [ ]   4 [ ] [ ] [ ]

**MIND TWISTERS, PUZZLES & GAMES** present simple, present perfect

# 45 Crack the code

**1** Use the phrases below to write questions.

Your questions should begin: *Do you (ever)...?* and *Have you (ever) ....?*

Examples:

use / chatlines — *Do you ever use chatlines?*

lose / your mobile phone — *Have you ever lost your mobile phone?*

**Group 1**

cheat / in an exam
cook / at home
forget / to do your homework
go / to school on foot
listen / to classical music
meet / an American person
read / Harry Potter books
ride / a motorbike
shop / for food
steal / something from a shop
swim / at midnight
watch / films in English
win / a prize
write / a poem

**Group 2**

be / sent out of class
break / a window
eat / Chinese food
get / top marks in a test
go / to the cinema
make / your computer crash
not study / for a test
play / any sports
speak / in English outside class
stay / up all night
talk / to your friends during lessons
tell / lies to your parents
travel / by hovercraft
visit / the capital of another country

**2** You will now play a game where you ask questions and work out a code!

**MIND TWISTERS, PUZZLES & GAMES** past simple, present perfect

# 46 English humour

**1** Work in pairs. Match the beginnings of the jokes (1-7) with their endings (a-g).

1 *Teacher*: Frederick, this letter from your mother, it looks like your handwriting.

   *Pupil*: ..................................................................................................................................................

2 *Teacher*: Where's your homework on memory?

   *Pupil*: ..................................................................................................................................................

3 *Teacher*: Isabelle, you should have been here at 9 o'clock.

   *Pupil*: ..................................................................................................................................................

4 *Pupil*: Help, I've lost my memory.

   *Teacher*: When did this happen?

   *Pupil*: ..................................................................................................................................................

5 *Teacher*: You weren't at school last Friday, Thomas. I heard you were out playing football all day.

   *Pupil*: ..................................................................................................................................................

6 *Pupil*: Please Miss, there's something wrong with me, I can see into the future.

   *Teacher*: That's incredible. When did your problem start?

   *Pupil*: ..................................................................................................................................................

7 *Teacher*: Which country do you like the best?

   *Pupil*: Kyrgyzstan.

   *Teacher*: Can you spell it?

   *Pupil*: ..................................................................................................................................................

a) I *forgot / have forgotten* to take it home, so I couldn't do it.

b) I *changed / have changed* my mind, Spain.

c) It *started / has started* next Thursday.

d) That's because she *borrowed* / *has borrowed* my pen.

e) That's not true Miss, I *did not play / haven't played* football. I've got the cinema tickets to prove it.

f) When *did what happen / has what happened*?

g) Why, what *happened / has happened*?

1 [d]  2 [ ]  3 [ ]  4 [ ]  5 [ ]  6 [ ]  7 [ ]

**2** Now underline the correct form of the verbs in italics.

Then write the endings of the jokes in the spaces.

**MIND TWISTERS, PUZZLES & GAMES** present continuous, past simple

# 47 Shoe mystery

**1** Work in groups.

Can you solve this mystery?

A young woman buys a pair of new shoes. She goes to work and dies.

Look at the four pictures below and decide which one offers the best explanation for her death.
Then write the story, explaining why the new shoes were responsible for her death.

1

2

3

4

**2** Work in groups.

Read the stories written by the other groups. Decide whose is the best story.
Your teacher will then give you the solution.

**MIND TWISTERS, PUZZLES & GAMES**  should, need, going to

# 48 School facilities

**1) Work in groups.**

You are the governors of your school.
You have €10 to spend on making your school better.

Look at the list below and decide how best to spend your money.

|  | € cost |
|---|---|
| new computer room | 2 |
| exchange trips with schools in Great Britain and the USA | 1 |
| new language laboratory | 1 |
| new science laboratory | 2 |
| special school buses to take you to school | 1 |
| new school theatre and music rooms | 1 |
| new art / pottery centre | 1 |
| new gym with indoor tennis, football and swimming | 3 |
| extra school trips (one a month) | 1 |
| three more teachers (aged 21-25) | 2 |
| smaller classes so that there are 15 students in each class | 2 |
| new school canteen (where you can eat your lunch) | 1 |
| bigger playground area | 1 |
| new heating / air conditioning system | 1 |
| Total: | €20 |

**2) Work in groups.**

Now explain your choices to another group.

Example:

*We are going to have a new science laboratory so we can do more experiments.*

**MIND TWISTERS, PUZZLES & GAMES** past simple, past continuous

# 49 Logic games

**1** Put the verbs into the texts.

The verbs should be in the past simple (e.g. *she came*) or past continuous (e.g. *she was coming*).

**a)**

| 1 come | 2 go | 3 cook | 4 run | 5 look | 6 listen | 7 know |
| 8 tell | 9 tell | 10 know | 11 lie | 12 lie | 13 listen | 14 come |

A mother **(1)** ......*came*...... home from work one evening. She **(2)** .......................... into the kitchen where her husband **(3)** .......................... dinner. She could hear a CD playing in the next room. She **(4)** .......................... into the room and turned off the music. She then **(5)** .......................... at her two sons and two daughters, and asked angrily;

'Who **(6)** .......................... to an Eminem CD?'

'I wasn't,' said Julia, her elder daughter.

'It was one of the girls,' said Richard, her younger son.

'No it wasn't,' said Adrian, her elder son, 'it was Richard.'

'That's not true,' said Anna, her younger daughter.

The mother **(7)** .......................... that on this occasion three of her children **(8)** .......................... the truth because they always **(9)** .......................... the truth. But she also **(10)** .......................... that one of them **(11)** .........................., because that child always **(12)** .......................... .

So, who **(13)** .......................... to the CD when their mother **(14)** .......................... home?

**b)**

| 15 be | 16 walk | 17 blow | 18 pass | 19 pick | 20 belong | 21 give |

It **(15)** .......................... a windy day and ten people wearing hats **(16)** .......................... towards a supermarket. Suddenly the wind **(17)** .......................... all their hats off. A young girl, who **(18)** .......................... by, **(19)** .......................... up all the hats and without asking who the hats **(20)** .......................... to, **(21)** .......................... each person a hat.

What are the chances of exactly nine people getting their own hats back?

**2** Work in groups. Solve the two problems.

**MIND TWISTERS, PUZZLES & GAMES**  past simple

# 50 Alibi

**1** Look at the pictures below.

They tell the story of a DJ who murders his wife and thinks he has the perfect alibi. But something goes wrong and his alibi is blown!

Put the pictures in order (pictures 1, 10 and 11 are already in the correct order).

**2** Work in pairs. Decide what happened in picture 10.

Here's a clue: what did the DJ hear on the radio?

**MIND TWISTERS, PUZZLES & GAMES** past simple, past perfect

# 51 Barman

**1** **Look at the pictures.**

Why did the barman point a gun at the girl?
Why did the girl say 'thank you'?

To help you answer these questions, underline the correct form of the verb.

**a)** <u>Did the barman know</u> / Had the barman known the girl?

**b)** Did the barman see / Had the barman seen her before somewhere?

**c)** Did the girl ever go / Had the girl ever been to this bar before?

**d)** Did she only ask / Had she only asked for something to drink?

**e)** Were there / Had there been any other people in the bar at that moment?

**f)** Did the girl arrange / Had the girl arranged to meet someone else in the bar?

**g)** Was the girl / Had the girl been shocked when the barman pointed the gun at her?

**h)** Did the barman shoot / Had the barman shot the girl?

**i)** Was the girl / Had the girl been thirsty?

**j)** Did she want / Had she wanted to take some pills or medicine?

**k)** Did the girl have / Had the girl had another type of problem?

**l)** Did the girl ever have / Had the girl ever had this problem before?

**m)** Did the barman solve / Had the barman solved this problem when he pointed the gun at her?

**2** **Memorize some of the questions.**

Now cover the page and ask your teacher the questions.

# 52 Mysteries

**1** Work in groups. Here are some mysteries for you to solve.

**1** Emma wakes up in the middle of the night and smells smoke. She knows she is in danger from the fire. She does not try to leave the room where she is sleeping.

## Why?

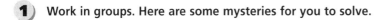

**2** Helena had not been seen for 24 hours. The police sent out a search party. They discovered her in a couple of hours covered in blood in an abandoned building. A few hours later, it was confirmed that she had been shot twice. Even though the police had no other physical evidence, they arrested the murderer.

## How did the police know the identity of the murderer?

**3** Teresa decides to buy a new stereo system and to sell her old one to a stranger. The stranger wants to pay in cash. Teresa accepts but says that the stranger must give her the money in front of a bank clerk in a bank.

## Why?

**4** Petra is talking to her lawyer in prison. They are both angry because the judge didn't grant bail. But at the end of their discussion, Petra is allowed to go home.

## Why?

**5** Mrs Smith, who lives alone with her daughter Natasha, suspects that Natasha's boyfriend has been staying in their house. But her daughter says that she has spent the day by herself and that her boyfriend was out with his friends. In reality, the boyfriend has spent the day in the house, so Natasha has made sure that he has not left anything behind. But Mrs Smith soon finds evidence that Natasha's boyfriend really has spent the day with Natasha in the house.

## What evidence does Mrs Smith find?

**2** Work in groups.

Here are ten solutions, but only five can be matched to the mysteries. Decide which ones can't go with any of the mysteries, and then which ones must go with one particular mystery.

- **a)** She was a police officer herself.
- **b)** She was alone.
- **c)** She lives next door to the bank.
- **d)** She is in a prison cell.
- **e)** She can smell perfume.
- **f)** She is blind.
- **g)** She wasn't dead when she was found. So she was able to reveal the identity of her killers.
- **h)** She sees that the toilet seat is up.
- **i)** She was only visiting.
- **k)** She kisses the guard.

1 ☐  2 ☐  3 ☐  4 ☐  5 ☐

**MIND TWISTERS, PUZZLES & GAMES** first conditional

# 53 Manager's dilemma

**1)** Look at these pictures.

Your teacher will tell a story. As you listen, put the pictures in the correct order.

a)

b)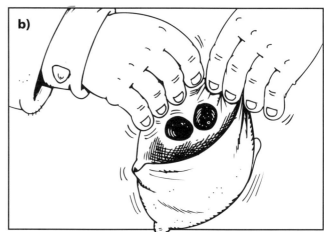

c)

d)

e)

f)

1 ☐   2 ☐   3 ☐   4 ☐   5 ☐   6 ☐

**2)** Work in groups. Can you think of a solution?

**3)** Write the whole story.

**MIND TWISTERS, PUZZLES & GAMES** second conditional

# 54 Enigmas

**1** Match the beginnings of these jokes with their punchlines.

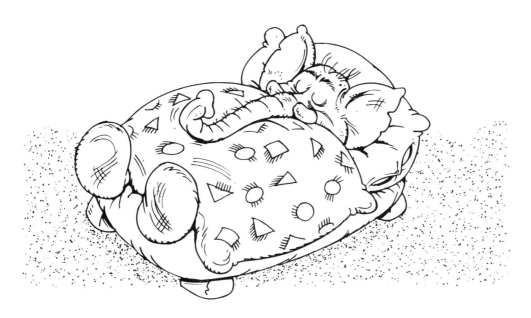

a) What would you do if you saw an elephant sleeping in your bed?

b) If you had five cakes and the boy next to you took three, what would you have?

c) Hugo, if you had ten euros and you gave five to your sister, what would you have?

d) If you had 100 dollars in one pocket and 50 dollars in the other pocket, what would you have?

e) If you saw something with two mouths, three noses and four eyes, what would you call it?

**1** Very very ugly.

**2** Ten euros. I don't have a sister.

**3** Sleep somewhere else.

**4** I would have the wrong clothes on.

**5** A big fight.

a ☐  b ☐  c ☐  d ☐  e ☐

**2** Work in groups.

Solve the brainteaser.

You are in the middle of the Sahara desert, dying of thirst. You meet two men who know where there is water. One of these men always tells the truth, the other always tells lies. What question would you ask one of them if you wanted to find out which was the road to water?

If you can't think of a solution, decide which of the three solutions below is the correct one.

a) Ask the one who tells the truth: 'If you were the liar, what would you say?' Then do what he says.

b) Ask the liar: 'What would you say?' Then do what he says.

c) Ask either the one who tells the truth or the liar: 'If you were him, what would you say?' Then do the opposite.

**Commissioning Editor:** Jacquie Bloese

**Project Editor:** Thérèse Tobin

**Designer:** Janet McCallum

**Illustrators:** Belinda Evans, David Farris

**Picture Editor:** Emma Bree

**Cover design:** Eddie Rego

**Photo credits**
Page 45: Hemera.

Mary Glasgow Magazines (Scholastic Inc.) grants teachers permission to photocopy the designated photocopiable pages from this book for classroom use. No other part of this publication may be reproduced in whole or in part, or stored in a retrieval system, or transmitted in any form or by any means, electronic, mechanical, photocopying, recording or otherwise, without written permission of the publisher.

For information regarding permission write to:
Mary Glasgow Magazines (Scholastic Inc.)
Commonwealth House
1-19 New Oxford Street
London WC1A 1 NU

© Mary Glasgow Magazines, an imprint of Scholastic Inc. 2004

All rights reserved.

Printed in the UK.